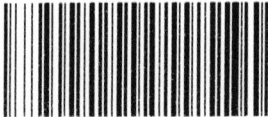

CW01465680

WHY SHOULD I GO TO BERLIN

WHY SHOULD I GO TO ↴

BERLIN

THE CITY YOU DEFINITELY NEED TO VISIT BEFORE YOU TURN 30

(m)

THIS IS WHY!

Berlin is a city of contrasts. It was once divided into East and West and traces of the division are still visible, whether you're just strolling the streets or visiting the various monuments. You'll find more museums scattered across the city than anywhere else in Europe and each one is worth the visit. But Berlin is also all about good yet affordable food, the best bars and yes, the techno scene is on the UNESCO cultural heritage list. The city's nightlife is legendary, with an eclectic array of bars, clubs, and music festivals for every genre and subculture.

Exploring this vibrant city doesn't have to break the bank. Walk, cycle, and use the U-Bahn if you don't want to miss out. Book a nice hostel, join free tours, and visit the most beautiful sights; there is a lot to see. You don't have to go up the Fernsehturm to enjoy it. Grab a bottle at one of the Spätis, get yourself a (vegan) *Döner*, have a picnic in one of the numerous parks, and immerse yourself in the local culture: there is something to suit every taste and budget.

Berlin stands for creativity, culture, and history but is modern nonetheless. From the colourful and buzzing areas of Kreuzberg and Neukölln to laid-back Mitte and Prenzlauer Berg, each Bezirk has its own distinctive character. We assure you: you'll feel at home everywhere. Keep on walking, take in the scenery, and soak up the atmosphere. One thing is certain: you will want to come back for more.

CONTENTS

DISTRICTS

Berlin is divided into twelve *Bezirke* or areas. We'll focus on the areas that are interesting for visitors who want to blend in with the locals, and where the famous Berlin vibe can be best experienced. Each area is divided into smaller parts, *Kiez*. In every chapter of this book, the addresses are arranged by the following areas.

Mitte

The city centre is called Mitte, literally meaning 'middle'. In Mitte you'll find the Reichstag, the Brandenburger Gate, the TV tower, and an abundance of shopping streets. Back in the days, half of Mitte was part of East Germany, half of it was West. If this is your first visit to Berlin, Mitte is where you should start.

WEDDING

PRENZLAUER
BERG

MITTE

FRIEDRICHSHAIN

CHARLOTTENBURG

KREUZBERG

SCHÖNEBERG

NEUKÖLLN

Prenzlauer Berg

Also known as Prenz'l Berg, it's one of the first areas where artists and young families started to settle after the fall of the Berlin wall in 1989, and therefore known as the place where gentrification started. You'll find a lot of nice shops, quiet cafés, bookshops, parks, and lovely restaurants in Prenzlauer Berg. And lots and lots of young children.

Friedrichshain

Best-known for the East Side Gallery, a popular tourist destination. We like to roam the flea market on Boxhagenerplatz on Sundays. Go to Simon-Dach-Strasse for bars and cafés, as well as affordable restaurants. Volkspark Friedrichshain is nice if you need a bit of green, but we also like to walk along the river Spree. Don't forget to check out R.A.W. Gelände (see page 63).

Kreuzberg

This part of town is split in two: Kreuzberg 36 and Kreuzberg 61, with the latter being a residential area. The magic happens at 36: street art, a lively club scene, lots of cool places and nice parks, markets, and much more. We love the alternative vibe of Kreuzberg and the range of things to do.

Neukölln

Located very close to Kreuzberg (meeting at the middle at Kreuzkölln), this area is lively and diverse, housing a large Turkish community. You'll find a lot of street art and a good vibe. It's also the area where you find Berlin's largest open space Tempelhofer Feld and (vintage) markets along the Maybachufer.

Charlottenburg

Historical, *schick* (chic) and very classy, Charlottenburg in a few words. You'll find many theatres, museums, and restaurants. Don't miss Kurfürstendamm, one of the most famous shopping streets (with mainly chains), or head to Charlottenburg Palace instantly.

Schöneberg

From the place where J.F.K.'s famous words "Ich bin ein Berliner" were spoken, to the heart of the Berlin gay scene (Nollendorfplatz), Schöneberg is very diverse.

Wedding

Multicultural Wedding, north of Mitte and Prenzlauer Berg, is an ever-upcoming area of the city. The neighbourhood is still quite affordable, and there are lots of creative spots. Vagabund Brauerei and Eschenbräu are two breweries where you can drink and eat. Or have a meal at Café Pförtner, in an old bus along the river Panke. Or just have a stroll along the river.

PRACTICAL
INFO

TRAVEL

Walking is a good way to explore Berlin: the pavements are wide, and just strolling through a city, being able to stop wherever you like, gives you the ultimate experience. However, as different areas of Berlin can be quite far apart and if you might not have a lot of time, you could take the S-Bahn (tram) or U-Bahn (underground). Or rent a bike.

Berlin's main central train station is Hauptbahnhof. The station – one of the biggest in Europe – can be a bit overwhelming, with platforms on multiple floors and levels. But there are many screens and endless signs; if you check them, you won't get lost. If you're interested in exploring Eastern Europe, you can catch trains to Bratislava, Budapest, Vienna, Prague, Poznan, Gdansk, and Warsaw, which depart from here daily. For day trips to Leipzig or Dresden, *bahn.de* will show you the best ticket options. If you arrive at Hauptbahnhof at the start of your Berlin trip, take the S-Bahn into the city. Buses and trams depart just outside the station.

The U-Bahn (short for *Untergrundbahn*, the underground) has a blue sign with a white U on it. Together with the S-Bahn (short for *Stadtschnellbahn*, typically trams), with a green sign with a white S, form the main transportation network for both the city and the suburbs and surrounding area. As confusing as it might seem, the S-Bahn goes underground in some parts of the city. Buy your tickets at ticket vending machines (cash or card) in the station. Some stations have service points. The fastest way is to download the BVG App and buy the tickets for instant or

later use. Always validate your tickets beforehand. There are no gates or turnstiles at the stations, but there are regular ticket inspections on the U- and S-Bahn.

There are multiple ticket types to choose from. For longer trips, you could buy the 7-day ticket to cover your fares. With the Berlin WelcomeCard you'll have one or two days of public transport, as well as discounts on sights and attractions.

Bus 100 was the first bus to connect the former East and West after the fall of the Wall and acts as a low-budget tourist bus. The first stop is Alexanderplatz. After that, you'll ride along the Berliner Dom, Reichtstag, Schloss Bellevue, Siegessäule, the Kaiser Wilhelm Gedächtniskirche, and the bus trip ends at Zoölogischer Garten, the zoo. Bus 200 takes about the same route but travels south from Tiergarten Park and will stop at Potsdamer Platz and the Holocaust Monument.

Renting a bike is a pleasant way of moving around any city. Berlin has many bike sharing services such as Bolt, Donkey Republic, LimeBike, Nextbike, and Tier. You'll come across many groups with yellow signs on their bikes, they are on guided tours with Berlin on Bike (*berlinonbike.de*).

WHERE TO STAY

The Circus Hostel

Weinbergsweg 1a, 10119
Mitte, circus-berlin.de

In Mitte, The Circus Group offer three options: a hostel, a hotel, and apartments. Depending on your budget, any option is good. The hostel offers beds in dorms for eight or ten: a bunk bed with some privacy and a private locker. The Circus Hostel (address below) is close to U-Bahnhof Rosenthaler Platz, and the hostel has a microbrewery in the basement. Need we say more?

Generator

staygenerator.com

This well-known worldwide chain of hostels has three locations in Berlin: Alexanderplatz, Mitte and Prenzlauer Berg. If you're not looking for the dorm experience, you can book a Single Pod with a very special bed of your own.

Meininger

meininger-hotels.com

On six locations in Berlin – with one at the airport – there is always room for you. And we like its vibrant colours. Meininger offers single and double rooms, multi-bedrooms, family rooms, and dorms. The best locations for a city trip are Hotel Berlin East Side Gallery (Friedrichshain), Berlin Alexanderplatz (Mitte), or Oranienburgerstrasse (Humboldthaus, Mitte).

St Christopher's Inns

st-christophers.co.uk

An international chain of hostels, with three options in Mitte. They offer private and shared rooms with a great view. The rooftop terrace in Mitte is legendary.

Heart of Gold Hostel

Johannisstrasse 11,
10117 Mitte,
heartofgold-hostel.de

Colourful rooms, a lot of bunk beds but also private rooms: generally, what you'd expect from a hostel. This one is located in a quiet street near the busy Oranienburgerstrasse. If you don't want to share a bathroom, you can book a private cabin. To love: the calendar that shows the cheaper and not so cheap dates.

Pfefferbett Hostel

Christinenstrasse 18-19,
10119 Prenzlauer Berg,
pfefferbett.de

Single rooms, double rooms, four-bedrooms, six-bedrooms, and a six-bedroom for girls only. Pfefferbett was once a brewery, founded in 1842. With an industrial atmosphere, it is great for those who don't want to spend lots on their bed as well as those who want to stay at a central location. S-Bahn and U-Bahn are around the corner. The hostel also has an entrance at Schönhauser Allee 176.

Kiez Hostel

Marchlewskistrasse 88,
10243 Friedrichshain,
kiezhostel.berlin

Rooms for two, but if you want to bring an extra friend (or some more: some rooms are for up to eight people), there's no issue at all. The Kiez Hostel offers thirteen rooms, most of them very colourful. Its perfect location is next to S+U-Bahnhof Warschauer Strasse. No rooms available? Try the nearby Sunflower Hostel. And do visit the bookshop Shakespeare & Sons around the corner.

Comebackpackers

Adalbertstrasse 97
10999 Kreuzberg,
comebackpackers.com

At Kottbusser Tor, you'll find a cosy hostel. Not a 'hotel-hostel', but a 'hostel-hostel' as they phrase it themselves. It's run by two friends who travelled the world, so you'll find all you need. Bedrooms and a large common room, what else is there?

Hüttenpalast

Hobrechtstrasse 66,
12047 Neukölln,
huettenpalast.de

Looking for something different? Book a caravan or hut at Hüttenpalast, an indoor camping site. The price for a caravan ranges from 70 to 100 euros for two, and there are options for three or four people. Plain old normal hotel rooms are also available. The hotel is split up in three sections and located in a classic *Hinterhoffabrik* (factory courtyard). Book on time, as this is a popular spot.

AMANO Hotels

amanogroup.com

No hostel pricing, but if you have just a tiny bit more to spend: the Amano chain has great rooms for fair prices. The rooftop terrace at the Amano in Auguststrasse is great in summer. Various hotels in Mitte, close to U-Bahn stations.

Michelberger Hotel

Warschauer Strasse 39-40, 10243 Friedrichshain, michelbergerhotel.com

Very cool rooms in a very cool hotel; very Instagrammable. Not the cheapest, but worth it. With a nice bar and restaurant. Go for the brunch menu; it's huge, and you won't need any food for the rest of the day.

Bikini Berlin

Budapester Strasse 40, 10787 Charlottenburg, 25-hours-hotels.com

If you want to stay the night at a special hotel. Overlooking the zoo and close to Kurfursten-damm, right in the heart of Charlottenburg, you'll find Bikini Berlin. Don't let the regular room prices frighten you: there are good online offers. If you can't afford the rooms, make sure to go for a drink at the Monkey Bar, or have dinner at Neni.

↓ MICHELBERGER HOTEL

GOOD TO KNOW

Language

Evidently, German is the main language in Berlin. Most people will be able to answer in English though but try to use some German. Unlike in a lot of other countries, not all people who work in hospitality are exchange students. It is appreciated if you try speaking German. Key is to be polite: if you would like (to order) something, *ich hätte gerne* (I would like to have) is so much nicer than *ich will* (I want). Practise some words (we love Duolingo) or stick to a simple *Es tut mir leid, ich spreche kein Deutsch* (I'm sorry, I don't speak German).

Cash

There are still lots of places that don't accept cards.

Make sure you have plenty of smaller banknotes, and some change as well. Ensure that you know exactly where to find a cashpoint or *Geldautomat* because in some areas there aren't that many. Try to get your cash from a bank cashpoint rather than one outside a hotel, or you'll pay extra for each withdrawal.

Museums

For under 18s, most museums are free. If you're 18+ and planning to visit a lot of museums during your stay, the 3-day Museum Pass Berlin is a very good option. There are sadly no special student fees. Student cards are only accepted for discounts for groups accompanied by a lecturer or professor. But the first Sunday of each month, all museums are free so if you plan your trip right, you might save a lot of money. Most museums are closed on Mondays and open on Sundays.

Shopping hours

Most shops open around 9 or 10am. Shops in the larger and main shopping streets are usually open from 10am to 8pm. Some shops in Mitte open at 11am or 12 noon and close at 8pm. Almost all shops are closed on Sundays, except for a few supermarkets in the larger train and U-Bahn stations (such as Hauptbahnhof and Ostbahnhof). Sunday Shopping happens eight times a year, two of which during Advent (the last four Sundays before Christmas).

No pictures, please!

Germans like their privacy. Taking photos in bars and clubs is highly frowned upon if not outright prohibited. When taking photos, even outside, make sure not to have strangers in frame and avoid using the flash altogether. Keep the pictures to you and your friends, sleeping cats or the sunset.

Eating habits

Breakfast or *Frühstück* is a very important meal in Germany, just a coffee and a bit of bread won't do. So, head for a place where you can have an extensive breakfast with eggs, various cheeses and meats, fresh fruit, et cetera. And lots of bread of course: German bread is the best in the world.

Lunch is important too, and usually hot. Eating a hot lunch is a lot cheaper than you might think. A lot of Berliners go out for a simple pasta, with spaghetti Bolognese being a favourite all over town.

In the afternoon, it is customary to have cake with your coffee: *Kaffee und Kuchen*. Sometimes the slices of cake are so big, you won't be hungry until late in the evening. A simple *Kuchen* is

often something simpler, like an apple crumble cake. *Torte* is German for fancy cakes, topped with fruit and cream. Good cakes can be eaten at bakeries and many specialised shops.

Traditionally, in Germany dinner is the *Abendbrot* (evening bread): bread with different types of cheese, sausages, raw vegetables, and the like. This is somewhat old fashioned: if you had a hot lunch, it wasn't considered necessary to eat a second hot meal. Due to changing eating habits and a more Mediterranean diet, more and more Germans tend to eat a hot meal in the evening as well.

Tipping

One of our favourite sayings in German: *Er hat einen Igel in der Tasche* (literally: He has a hedgehog in his pocket, meaning that he is not a big spender and/or a lousy tipper). To not be a Scrooge would be our advice. Tipping is not obligatory but highly appreciated. You'd want to tip about 5 to 10% in a restaurant or bar. Tour guides expect a tip of around 10%. And if you take a taxi, always round up the bill.

Going to a *Kneipe*

There are a few things to remember when going to a bar. If you order a beer without specifying what you want, you will receive half a litre of Pilsner in most places. Cash is king at most bars, so do not expect to be able to pay by card. Non-smokers beware: many bars in Berlin are smoking bars. As bars stay open longer, Berliners tend to leave their home later: do not be surprised if you find a bar practically empty at 7pm on a Friday night. Always have photo ID on you in the city: you might need it at a bar. Unlike in other European countries, you can drink beer or wine from 16.

Berlin's nightlife scene is known for its techno clubs and (illegal) raves and is often called the techno capital of the world. The fall of the Berlin Wall in 1989 allowed for the rising popularity of techno, and it's only grown from there. Whether you've ever been to a techno party or not, we highly recommend checking out the iconic party scene while you can. See page 133 for our favourite clubs.

BERLIN IN SPRING

Our favourite season! Berlin in spring is wonderful: after a very long and dark winter, everybody seems happy that the sun is out again, and the days are getting longer. Berlin is always lovely, but especially in spring.

After the Fall of the Wall, Japan donated a lot of cherry trees to the city of Berlin. They were planted all over the city. There is even a whole street dedicated to them: the TV-Asahi-Kirschblütenallee (take the S-Bahn to Lichterfelde Süd). Some other beautiful spots to visit, with or without the trees blossoming, are Schwedter Strasse near Mauerpark and Monbijou Park near the Museumsinsel.

Also better when the sun is out: having drinks and meeting people in one of the many *Biergärten* in the city (see page 105), where you can have a drink and a small snack while sitting under the trees, enjoying the first rays of sunshine.

On International Women's Day (8th March) people in Berlin have a day off, unlike the rest of the country where it is not an official holiday. Don't be surprised if you're offered a flower by a stranger if you are a woman. Since 1911, it has been celebrated annually, with women in Germany receiving the right to vote seven years later, at the dawn of the Weimar Republic. Another official day of celebration, and of protest, is Labour Day on 1st May.

BERLIN IN SUMMER

For most Berliners, summer means leaving the city. If you're going in summer, make sure to pack a bathing suit, beach towel, and loads of sunscreen. Pick one of the many lakes surrounding the city or find inspiration on *takemetothelakes.com*. Most are accessible by S-Bahn, but you could rent a bike and enjoy the ride out of the city. Go swimming at Krumme Lanke in Grunewald Forest, take a plunge in Schlachtensee, head for Tegelersee or Weissensee. There are many more, simply pick the closest.

If you prefer swimming in an outdoor pool, check out Badeschiff in the Spree River (*arena.berlin*). It has a beach bar and is one of the best urban pools we have ever come across. The view over the river is beautiful, especially when facing the statue *Molecule Man*, a little further to the east in the middle of the river.

Summer is also festival season, just check *visitberlin.de* or *berlin.de* – there is just too much to choose from. Berlin Fashion Week is in July as well in January. Beer geeks can visit the Beer Festival in Friedrichshain, which is spread over 2km+ between Strausberger Platz and Frankfurter Tor. Many beer producers from all over the world present their products for you to taste.

BERLIN IN AUTUMN

From September to October the beloved Festival of Lights takes place: where many landmarks and buildings are illuminated in creative ways. Try to visit Museumsinsel during this festival when Berliner Dom is one of the main spectacles.

The reunification of Germany is celebrated on 3rd October. Every 9th November, the Fall of the Wall is celebrated. Each year, gatherings are held at the former border checkpoints, and museums hold dedicated exhibitions. Every five years, celebrations garner a bit more attention.

One of the bigger events in autumn is the Berlin Marathon, which attracts over 45,000 athletes from all over the world. During the event, the city is crowded – hotels and hostels will be full and more expensive for it. Check the exact date beforehand to keep in mind for your booking. Or start your training and join in! The half-marathon takes place in spring.

Nature lovers, prepare yourself for beautiful colours in Berlins many parks. They make for a dramatic background in your city trip pictures. It can be a bit chilly in autumn, but September and October are mostly still a bit warm.

BERLIN IN WINTER

Berlin in winter is cold and often dark, but also magical. Bring a hat, gloves, and a warm coat and sturdy shoes. Yes, we may sound like your parents, but it gets *really* cold, especially in the evenings. Every neighbourhood has its own Christmas market (*visitberlin.de*), most of them very German with lots of *Glühwein* (mulled wine), *Stollen* (almond-spiced bread with dried fruits) and *Bratwurst* but there are themed markets as well. One of our favourites is the Lucia Christmas Market (*lucia-weihnachtsmarkt.de*) in Kulturbrauerei in Prenzlauer Berg. Lucia is the Norwegian goddess of light: the market is all about the Nordics.

Ice rinks are all over town, and skates can be rented everywhere. We like the ones at the Christmas Market at Potsdamer Platz, the ice rink around the Neptune statue close to the Fernsehturm or the Erika Hess Ice Stadium in Wedding. There are many more to be found on websites like *exberliner.com* or *visitberlin.de*. We highly recommend YAAM on Ice. YAAM stands for Young African Art Market and is currently located (its future is sadly uncertain) at An der Schillingbrücke 3 in Friedrichshain

If you're seeking something special and have the money to spend, head for Cafe am Neuen See in Tiergarten Park to go Eisstock-schiessen, a nice mix of curling and jeu-de-boules.

Film lovers won't miss the Berlinale. The famous film festival is one of the biggest in the world and attracts many visitors. The festival usually takes place in February and goes back to 1951, when it was used as a 'showcase of the free world'. You'll find info and tickest on *berlinale.de*.

BERLIN LIFE

HISTORY

Attempting to cover all of Berlin's history in just a few pages is frankly impossible, we could write a 400-page book about just the DDR-era, (the time of the Deutsche Demokratische Republik, in English known as GDR) . However, you can't visit Berlin without delving just a little bit into history as knowing some of its background will make your trip much more interesting.

Origins of Berlin

Berlin started out as a little place in the marshlands of what is now the State of Brandenburg. The city's first mention on record was in 1237 but had been there for centuries. Germany has not always been Germany, nor has Berlin always been the capital. Berlin was the capital of the Margraviate of Brandenburg, the Kingdom of Prussia, the German Empire, the Weimar Republic, Nazi Germany, East Germany (the DDR – during this period, Bonn was the capital of the BRD, West Germany) and finally, since 1990, the capital of reunited Germany.

Berliner Bär

While many perceive Ampel-männchen as Berlin's emblem – with many tourists buying a tote or a key ring with it – Berlin's true city crest is the bear. As the legend goes, in the 12th century a man called Albrecht der Bär (*Bär* also meaning bear) was on a hunt in the area that is now Berlin. He killed a bear and decided to stay and build a village. In the 13th century, the bear was depicted in the emblem of the army of the Margraviate of Brandenburg. Many centuries later, the bear is everywhere: you'll see statues and sculptures of it, it shows on memorials, beer brands, you name it ...

Napoleon

One of the most famous Berlin landmarks is Brandenburger Tor, or Brandenburger Gate. It was built in the late 18th century. The quadriga, a chariot driven by four horses, has been on top since its construction. Although Napoleon stole the quadriga in 1806 and took it to Paris, it was returned in 1814 by a German marshal and placed back on top of the gate (see page 48).

U-Bahn

Modern as it may seem, the first U-Bahn line (number 1, naturally) opened in 1902 and ran between Stralauer Tor and Potsdamer Platz. Other lines were soon added afterwards,

the last one (U8) in 1927. All were extended over the years. Stations each have their own architecture, contain murals, and even art installations. Some people make their own artwork by stopping at every single station, taking a picture, and moving along: 'only 172 more stops to go!'

Weimar Republic

After World War I and the abdication of Kaiser Wilhelm II in 1918, Germany was introduced to democracy for the very first time, with the Weimar Republic (1919-1933). As in most parts of the Western world, Germany was experiencing an economic crisis as well as a cultural and intellectual rise, with a vibrant bar and club scene. The German Expressionist movement produced some of the most impressive films of the time, with the movement's core in Berlin. Some of these movies are still shown at film

festivals and art house cinemas (see pages 66-67 for Kino International and Babylon Berlin).

Bauhaus

The famous art school Bauhaus was founded in Weimar but moved to Berlin in 1932. It was founded by Walter Gropius, who aimed to integrate crafts, arts, and technology. Their key phrase was 'form follows function': all designs had to be practical. The movement existed only from 1919 to 1933, before the Nazi regime suppressed it, but is still influential. If you want to know more about the movement, visit the Bauhaus Museum in Berlin or go to Dessau (the building is a UNESCO World Heritage site), a two-hour train ride from Hauptbahnhof.

The Third Reich

The darkest chapter in German history is the Third Reich, the period during which Hitler was its dictator, from 1933 to his suicide in 1945 – he died in his own bunker in Berlin, where he had been hiding. Under his leadership, the Second World War broke out, and millions of Jews and other minorities were murdered. Two impressive memorial sites in Berlin commemorate World War II and Nazi cruelties: museum Topographie des Terrors and the Holocaust Monument.

1936 Summer Olympics

One of the most controversial Olympic Games ever, but also the first to be broadcast on television. Hitler attempted to use the games as Nazi propaganda, trying to promote of Aryan supremacy. African American athlete Jesse Owens participated in the event against advice, and subsequently won four gold medals, foiling Hitlers plans by being the single most successful athlete at the event and clearly not Aryan. The Olympic stadium is now a venue for concerts and football matches, but it also hosts a memorial for Jesse Owens. Take the U2 to Olympiastadion to visit it.

The Cold War

After 1945, Berlin was divided into four sectors. They were controlled by the Americans, French, British, and Russians respectively, with West Berlin as the western enclave. Checkpoint Charlie is probably the most famous border crossing, where at one point in time tanks stood opposite each other. Very frightening at the time, nowadays merely a tourist attraction. Despite all this, Berlin's cultural scene was very much alive during the Cold War. Many artists lived in Berlin in the 70s, including David Bowie and Iggy Pop.

Escaping the East

Many people tried to go over the Wall between 1961 and 1989. Perhaps you've seen the famous picture of Conrad Schumann, an East German soldier who jumped over a barbed wire fence just days before construction of the wall. At the spot where he jumped into the free West, at the crossing of Bernauer Strasse and Ruppiner Strasse, you can learn more about the wall (see page 51). Right until the moment the Wall came down, he was afraid that the Stasi (the Eastern secret police) would come after him, but that never happened: 'It was only after 9 November 1989 that I felt truly free.'

Ghost stations

During the Cold War, the city was not only divided above ground but also underground. No less than sixteen underground stations

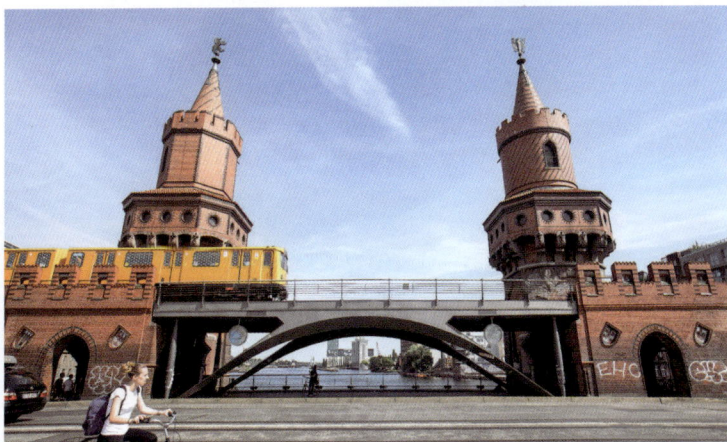

from the S-Bahn and U-Bahn were not accessible for people from both the West and East. Trains from 'the other side' would slowly pass these guarded stations, which gave passengers an uneasy feeling, resulting in the name ghost stations. At the train station Nordbahnhof (near Bernauer Strasse) you can visit a small exhibition about these stations.

Ampelmännchen

The cute little green and red guys on the traffic lights are called Ampelmännchen (Little traffic light men). They were invented by an East German traffic psychologist who wanted to create a friendly traffic light that people would actually take note of. It became a symbol of the DDR and has become a beloved sign. Nowadays, you can find Ampelmännchen in other parts of Berlin, and even other German cities. There is a tourist shop at Unter den Linden (as well as three other locations in town) where you can buy lots of souvenirs with the green (and red) men on it.

A lot of green

Berlin is one of the greenest cities in Europe. Nice to know: every Berliner has the right to 6 m2 of green space within a 500-metre distance from where they live. Especially in the former East there are many small parks between blocks of houses. Those patches of green, many including playgrounds, are still quite nice to relax in. After World War II, the Soviet Union lacked the funds to restore or rebuild the destroyed houses in their sector. At the same time, the Western half of Berlin invested a lot of money into new infrastructure. This discrepancy is still visible and quite clear, with more older buildings (now restored) in the Eastern half and more modern buildings in the West.

Cobblestones

The Berlin Wall was not just a wall: the DDR side included a so-called dead strip. This construction is best seen at Bernauer Strasse. In the streets, you'll see a double row of cobblestones marking the former wall over a length of almost 6 kilometres. New buildings are built over it, so sometimes the stones stop quite abruptly. If you want to make sure you see them, head for Brandenburger Tor or Potsdamer Platz. It is strange that we can now so easily cross the stones, while there was once a time when this was completely unfathomable.

Football

One of the most popular sports in Germany. Their oldest football club is BFC Germania, founded in 1888, but it's not as famous as Hertha BSC (short for Berliner Sport-Club) or 1. FC Union Berlin. Matches are mostly held in the Olympic Stadium. Germany is one of the most successful teams in World Cup history: the men have won the cup four times (1954, 1974, 1990, and 2014) and the women twice (2003 and 2007). The Olympiastadium is home to Hertha BSC, and purchasing tickets on the website is straightforward and not as expensive as you might expect for a Bundesliga team.

SIGHTSEEING

Brandenburger Tor

Pariser Platz, 10117 Mitte

This icon was built in the 18th century. It was designed to look like a Roman gate, but it resembles a Greek building, a style once very popular in Berlin. On top of the gate stands a chariot drawn by four horses, a so-called quadriga. The Tor was the symbol of the Nazi party until 1945, and during the Cold War it served as the border between the Russian and American sections of the city. When the Berlin Wall fell in 1989 it became a symbol for freedom. Nowadays, a lot of demonstrations as well as parties are held around the Tor.

Checkpoint Charlie

Friedrichstrasse 43-45, 10117 Mitte

The Russian section in Berlin had many borders with the French, American, and English sections. Best known and most photographed must be Checkpoint Charlie, where soldiers stood nose-to-nose for many months. In 1961, tanks literally stood opposite each other. It was the only crossing point for foreigners, which you could pass either on foot or by car.

Holocaust Monument

Cora-Berliner Strasse 1, 10117 Mitte

Officially, this monument is called *Memorial to the Murdered Jews of Europe*. The over 2,700 grey concrete slabs, different in size and height, stand in an almost 2,0000 m2 area in the heart of Berlin next to Brandenburger Tor and close to Tiergarten Park. Walking through the stones is permitted, and it will give you a feeling of loss and disorientation. It was opened in 2005, sixty years after the end of World War II. Be respectful of the site and keep its name in mind: don't walk on the stones, have picnics on them, or use them as a meaningless backdrop to selfies. Below the memorial – not everybody knows this – you'll find an underground information centre.

Karl-Marx-Allee

Karl-Marx-Allee, Mitte / Friedrichshain

You might question what could be special about an Allee, or avenue. Karl-Marx-Allee was built in the 1950s and once called Stalinallee. It is a great example of socialist architecture: grand façades, impressive residential buildings, alongside offices and cultural institutes. You'll find iconic symbols of the DDR era on the Allee:

↓ BRANDENBURGER TOR

↓ FERNSEHTURM

Strausberger Platz and Frankfurter Tor. You can see a flash of the Allee in *The Queen's Gambit*: although the story took place in Russia and the USA, the Netflix series was mainly filmed in Berlin. Tip: When you stand in the middle of the Allee you'll be able to take the perfect snap of the Fernsehturm (TV Tower).

Reichstag

Platz der Republik 1, 10111 Mitte

As most of the city, the Reichstag is a symbol of German history. In 1933 the building was destroyed by a fire and left unused until the reunification in 1990. Since then, it has housed German parliament, known as *Bundestag*. The DDR government was housed in the Palast der Republik, which was demolished in 2003. You can visit the Reichstag and its glass dome for free but must register in advance. There is a rooftop restaurant where you could have breakfast, lunch, or dinner, but it is quite pricey.

Fernsehturm

1 Panoramastrasse 1a, 10178 Mitte

The iconic TV Tower in East Berlin was built between 1965 and 1969. At 368 metres, it is one of the tallest towers in Europe. Its main function is transmitting tv and radio signals. You can go up the tower and visit the restaurant, and best of all: enjoy the view across the city. You can't visit Berlin without taking a picture of it. It is a symbol of the DDR era, as it was built during the Cold War.

**Gedenkstätte
Berliner Mauer**

*Bernauer Strasse 111,
13355 Mitte*

The Gedenkstätte, or Berlin Wall Memorial, stretches 1.4 kilometres along the former border between East and West Berlin. Walk along an outdoor exhibition, a wheatfield (part of the *Parliament of Trees*, an art installation by Ben Wagin also commemorating the Wall), and the rebuilt Chapel of Reconciliation. The original chapel from 1894 was demolished to make place for wall fortifications.

East Side Gallery

*Mühlenstrasse, 10243
Friedrichshain / Kreuzberg*

This piece of the Berlin Wall is not only a memorial but also the longest street art gallery in the world, spanning 1.2 kilometres. It is worth the visit. The wall shows famous murals, such as *My God, Help Me to Survive This Deadly Love* by Dmitri Vrubel. This depicts Soviet politician Brezhnev and the German communist General

CHECKPOINT CHARLIE

↓ GEDÄCHTNISKIRCHE

Secretary Honecker kissing, a reproduction of the kiss given in 1979 at the foundation of the DDR. Another famous piece is *Test the Best*, a mural of a Trabant car going through the Wall. The East Side Gallery was created in 1990, has murals of over one hundred artists and has attracted millions of people over the years. The monument stands for freedom, mostly, and is open to visitors free of charge.

Gedächtniskirche

Breitscheidplatz, Charlottenburg

The centre of Charlottenburg houses an interesting church. Built in the 19th century, the Kaiser Wilhelm Memorial Church was built to commemorate this emperor. It was bombed during World War II and should have been demolished as it was extremely damaged. Instead, the city decided to keep it as a Memorial Hall for all the victims of the Second World War. Next to the Gedächtniskirche stands a new church. Both serve as reminders of the cruelties of the war.

MUSEUMS

Museumsinsel

Museumsinsel,
10178 Mitte,
museumsinsel-berlin.de

Museumsinsel, a UNESCO World Heritage Site in itself, contains five museums and a gallery. The **Alte Nationalgalerie** is filled with 19th century art. The **Altes Museum** is dedicated to archaeology, built in the early 19th century to house the art collection of the Prussian royal family. The round building of the **Bode-Museum** houses sculptures as well as paintings. The **Neues Museum** is home to many archaeology collections, with the bust of Nefertiti the most famous — and controversial: the Egyptian authorities have been asking for its return for over a century. Last, but not least, is the **Pergamon Museum**, also housing many antiquities. The large Pergamon altar is as beautiful as its place is controversial. On the other side of the water, you'll see a new building, the **James-Simon-Galerie**, by architect David Chipperfield.

Deutsches Historisches Museum

Unter den Linden 2, 10117
Mitte, dhm.de

Historical museums — boring? Not this one! Its exhibits are stunning most of the time and beautifully presented, even if you're not familiar with German history yet. For instance, the exhibit about turning points in German history, is presented backwards, traveling from 1989 (the revolution in the DDR) to 1848 (another revolution). You learn everything there is to know about one of the biggest countries in Europe.

↓ DEUTSCHES HISTORISCHES MUSEUM

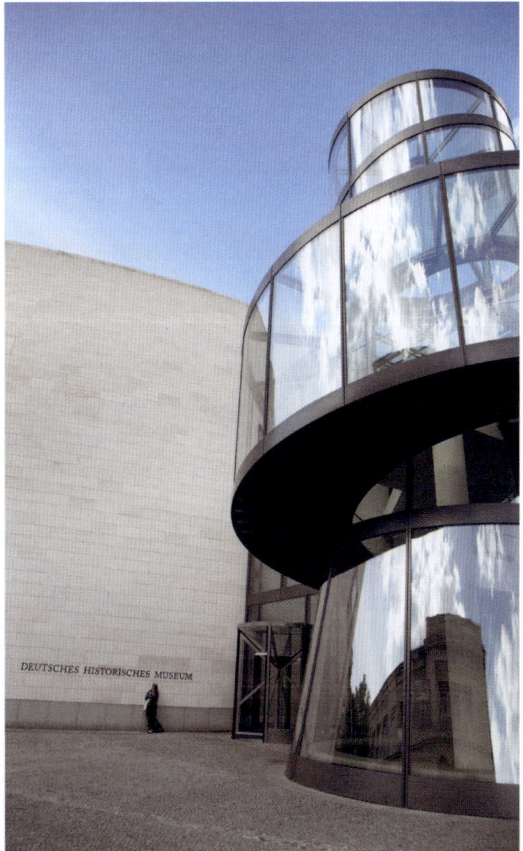

DEUTSCHES HISTORISCHES MUSEUM

Fotografiska Berlin

Oranienburger Strasse 54, Mitte, berlin.fotografiska. com

Fotografiska, with sister museums in Stockholm, New York, Tallinn, and Shanghai is a photography museum. Beautiful expositions, and a very nice restaurant on the fifth floor. It is one of the few museums that offer a discount if you're under 25, and it has cheaper rates on weekdays.

Gropius Bau

Niederkirch Strasse 7, 10963 Mitte, gropiusbau. de

They claim to be one of the most important exhibition halls of Europe, and they seem to be right. In the beautiful building of Gropius Bau, you can see some of the best exhibitions of contemporary art. Closed on Tuesdays.

Museum für Naturkunde

Invalidenstrasse 43, 10115 Mitte, museumfuernaturkunde. berlin

Visiting a museum for natural history is always a good idea, although the temporary exhibitions of the Museum für Naturkunde might be more for your younger siblings (dinosaurs!). Go in to see the taxidermy exhibit where Knut, the famous polar bear from the Berlin Zoo is now displayed. The insect models, made between 1930 and 1955 by preparator Alfred Keller, are very special. Reduced entrance for students.

Neue Nationalgalerie

Potsdamer Strasse 50, 10785 Mitte, smb.museum

Housed in a building (built between 1965 and 1968) by the famous architect Mies van der Rohe, which makes the visit to this museum for contemporary art even better. The collection includes art from the 20th century, with a focus on European and North American artists. Entrance is free for under 18s.

Topographie des Terrors

Niederkirchnerstrasse 8, 10963 Mitte, topographie. de

Both indoor and outdoor, this museum focuses on Berlin from 1933 to 1945: the SS and the terror of the Nazi oppression. The outdoor part of the museum is located at the former headquarters of the Third Reich. Free admission.

Tränenpalast

Reichstagufer 17, 10117 Mitte, hdg.de

One of the most impressive museums about the division of Berlin. At the time, at a few border points people could move from one side to the other. Meaning: West Berliners could visit their Eastern relatives, but not the other way around. The name Tränenpalast, meaning Palace of Tears, speaks for itself. You get a very good insight into how daily life must have been, you can feel how procedures worked, and even walk through an original passport check booth. Learn a lot about history by just visiting this small place. Entrance is free.

Computerspiele-museum

Karl-Marx-Allee 93a, 10243 Friedrichshain, computerspielemuseum.de

The only museum in the world dedicated to computer games. Want to know which games your parents played in the 80s and 90s? Visiting the Computerspielemuseum is like travelling back in time. Over 300 computer games are on display, and there is an arcade in 80s style.

Berlinische Galerie

Alte Jakobstrasse 124-128, 10969 Kreuzberg, berlinischegalerie.de

A beautiful museum for modern art created in Berlin. Expect fine arts, prints, and drawings but also a focus on architecture and photography. The building is modern, and in front of the entrance you'll see a yellow field with black letters, showing all the names of the 160 artists whose work is displayed. Free admission for under 18s, student discount.

↓ BERLINISCHE GALERIE

↓ C|O BERLIN

Bauhaus Archive

Klingelhöferstrasse 14, Tiergarten / Charlottenburg, 10785 bauhaus.de

As we are compiling this guide, the Bauhaus Archive is temporarily closed, and the collection has been moved to Knesebeckstrasse 1 in Charlottenburg. The museum has a lot to offer to Bauhaus enthusiasts; check the website for updates on the project.

C|O Berlin

Hardenbergstrasse 22, 10623 Charlottenburg, co-berlin.org

Amerika Haus is home to one of Berlin's photography museums, C|O Berlin. This great exhibition space supports new talent as well. There is a yearly talent award for photographers under 35 and its exhibition is always interesting. Check the website for dates and former winners. Thoroughly inspiring.

Helmut Newton Stiftung

Jebensstrasse 2, 10623 Charlottenburg, helmut-newton-foundation.org

Why have museum for an American photographer in Germany? Helmut Newton was actually born Helmut Neustädter, in Berlin in 1920. He is known for his photos of powerful female nudes but made a lot of other work. He photographed for magazines such as Vogue and Harper's Bazaar.

Schwules Museum

Lützowstrasse 73, Schöneberg, schwulesmuseum.de

This international centre for the culture and history of queer people (*schwules* meaning gay), hosts many exhibitions, a lot of them photography. Check the website to see what's on during your visit. Closed on Tuesdays. Student discount.

STREET ART

Berlin is the graffiti capital of Germany, maybe even of Europe. A lot of houses are completely covered in graffiti, often in an artistic way, at other times – not so much. There are many murals to see in Berlin. Although we found some of the best for you, we can't promise that they will all still be there when you visit.

Haus Schwarzenberg

Rosenthaler Strasse 39, 10178 Mitte, haus-schwarzenberg.org

Street art and history combined. Inside the Hackescher Höfe (Hacke's Courtyards) you'll find the famous Neurotitan Gallery in Haus Schwarzenberg. The outside walls are covered with great murals, such as a large piece portraying Anne Frank. Next to that mural, you'll find Anne Frank Zentrum, which hosts the exhibition *All about Anne*.

Mauerpark

Bernauer Strasse / Eberswalderstrasse, 10437 Prenzlauer Berg, mauerpark.info

This lovely park (see pages 140 & 170) is not just home to one of the largest flea markets in town, but also has a large strip of the wall left, which is a great graffiti spot. New artists frequently work on it, transforming the wall daily. The park is quite big. Take the U2 to Eberswalderstrasse or the M10 (tram) to Wolliner Strasse. Walk the Oderbergstrasse for the scenic route to the park.

East Side Gallery

*Mühlenstrasse, 10243
Friedrichshain, stiftung-
berliner-mauer.de*

The most famous location for graffiti. This is one of the few places artists are not supposed to work on anymore. Most murals are considered protected art since the gallery became a monument in 2018. Book a tour if you want to know all the ins and outs. (See page 70).

R.A.W. Gelände

*Revalerstrasse 99, 10245
Friedrichshain,
raw-gelaende.de*

A nice spot to visit in Friedrichshain is R.A.W. Gelände. R.A.W. is short for Reichsbahn-Ausbesserungs-Werk, Railway Repair Works, and it's on a former industrial site that has been there since 1867. Besides the many exhibitions, a skating hall, and clubs you can visit, the buildings are full of wall art.

Oberbaumbrücke

Mühlenstrasse, 10234
Friedrichshain

Once the only connection between Friedrichshain (East) and Kreuzberg (American sector), the Oberbaumbrücke is now the place to see some impressive murals. We especially like the *Yellow Man* by Os Gemeos at Oppelner Strasse 3.

Street Art Tour

Warschauerstrasse 54,
10243 Friedrichshain,
alternativeberlin.com

You'll find this one on page 70 as well, so we'll keep it short and sweet: Alternative Berlin organises street art tours around the city. The English tour takes three hours and costs 20 euros but is truly worth the money. Meet-up is at Snackbar Wursthain at R.A.W. Gelände.

Urban Nation

Bülowstrasse, 10783
Schöneberg, urban-
nation.com

Street art's natural habitat is of course the street, but Urban Nation is a museum dedicated to the art of murals. Many street artists made works specifically for the museum, which is a living object in itself. Its façade is different every time you visit.

Teufelsberg

Teufelsseechaussee
10, 14193 Grunewald,
teufelsberg-berlin.de

In addition to its historical significance, Teufelsberg, a former US listening station during the Cold War, is filled with graffiti. Over four hundred works can be seen, and new works are added almost every month. The view over the city is spectacular as well. You can find the Teufelsberg in Grunewald, a district and forest outside the city. Entrance with or without a guide is 5 euros.

CINEMA

A good idea on a rainy day: a trip to the cinema. Most movie theatres show films that are dubbed into German, but there still are many cinemas that show films in English. Check for the following abbreviations: OmU means original version with German subtitles; OmeU is the original version with English subtitles, OmU+ is subtitles in both English and German and OV is the original version, without any subtitles.

Babylon

*Rosa Luxemburg Platz 30,
10119 Mitte,
babylonberlin.eu*

A beautiful cinema in Mitte, opposite the Volksbühne theatre, built around 1928. The programme is far from the obvious blockbusters; you can watch the true classics here. They even show silent films, accompanied by the movie theatre organ and orchestra. The cinema's history is as turbulent as the rest of the city's. Babylon organises themed weeks, some film festivals, and more.

Hackesche Höfe Kino

Rosenthaler Strasse 40-41, 10178 Mitte, hoefekino.de

The Hackesche Höfe, the well-known courtyards in Mitte, are worth the visit, but it can get crowded when the shops are open. Buy cinema tickets, many international and independent movies are shown here, and art house is key. You shouldn't be afraid to climb some stairs, as the cinema has no lift. If your German is good enough, read the funny FAQ section on the website.

Kino International

Karl-Marx-Allee 33, 10178 Mitte, yorck.de

The grandest cinema of Berlin: it has the looks of a Wes Anderson film set, built in the 60s during the DDR era. And it is located on one of the most impressive streets of the city as well. The Yorck Kinogruppe has several beautiful cinemas spread over town, and most show the films in the original language.

Kino in der Kulturbrauerei

Schönhauser Allee 36, 10435 Prenzlauer Berg, cinestar.delucernaire.fr

Location is key, with this cinema in the middle of the charming Kulturbrauerei. The cinema itself is – to be very honest – a regular cinema that happens to show a lot of movies in the original version. Cinestar has four more cinemas in Berlin, located in rather uncharming buildings but once inside that problem is solved of course.

FESTIVALS

Atonal

berlin-atonal.com

The famous festival for experimental music and art returned in 2023 after a two-decade break. That edition was described as 'multifocal, alien, alive'. You can check for yourself what this means during two weekends in September.

Berlinale

berlinale.de

Officially named Berlinale International Film Festival, this is one of the biggest film festivals in Europe. It shows over four hundred films each year, from all over the world. It usually takes place in February. Films are shown on various locations in town, tickets are available only three days in advance so make sure you put it in your calendar.

Christopher Street Day Parade

csd-berlin.de

This parade is named after the New York street that has been the epicentre of the world's gay rights movement since the 1970s. This colourful parade celebrates LGBTQI+ people and their allies. It has taken place in Berlin every July since 1979. June and July mark Pride Month in Berlin. Check the website for additional events such as film screenings and parties.

Fête de la Musique

fetedelamusique.de

Any musician can participate at this festival. Small stages, big stages, on the website you can find the matchmaking tool: Tinder for musicians. If you just want to have a listen, come to Berlin on 21st June: the beginning of summer and the longest day of the year.

Internationales Literaturfestivald

literaturfestival.com

A highly enjoyable literary festival, even if you don't speak any German: as its name Internationales Literaturfestival suggests, it is an international event. The festival takes place in September and has one day dedicated to graphic novels.

Karneval der Kulturen

karneval.com

Whitsunday weekend is the time for the multicultural festival Karneval der Kulturen. Get ready for colourful processions led by people from Germany, as well as South America and Africa. Participants wear beautiful costumes and have a lot of fun. There are many musical and theatrical performances as well. The festival goes on for four days.

Krake Festival

krake-festival.de

A festival all about electronic music in the Summer. The date is announced on the website each year, as well as its locations. Wondering about the nice-looking octopuses on the website? *Krake* is German for octopus.

Lollapalooza

lollapaloozade.com

One weekend in September, usually the first, is all about Lollapalooza. It is one of the largest music festivals in Europe. Great bands, singers, and songwriters perform on stage at Olympiastadion and Olympiapark.

TOURS

Alternative Berlin Tours

Alternativeberlin.com

Book The Real Berlin Experience or a Street Art Tour. The tours take two to four hours, and all you have to bring is an AB Day ticket for the S- and U-Bahn. Your guide knows all about the city there is to know, and the twenty euro fee is worth every cent. The Free Tour is indeed free but always remember to tip your guide. If you're in Berlin with a group of students, consider the Alternative Student Tour. All tours start in Mitte or Friedrichshain.

Berlin on Bike

Knaackstrasse 97, 10435 Prenzlauer Berg, berlinonbike.de

You can either rent a bike and explore the city yourself, or book a tour with an English, German or even Dutch-speaking guide. There are several options, and most tours are 12 to 15 kilometres. One of the options is a tour focusing on Berlin's Cold War history. If you are visiting the city with your family or a larger group of friends, opt for the private tour. Prices vary depending on the tour and date; check the website for details.

Berliner Unterwelten

Badstrasse / Behmstrasse,
13357 Gesundbrunnen,
berliner-unterwelten.de

Save this tour for an extremely hot or a rainy day: you're going underground, either with a guide or independently. Make sure to wear appropriate footwear: avoid flip flops, high heels, and sandals. You can choose from various tours that start at different locations, but you will mostly be visiting old bunkers. One of them is the biggest bunker in Berlin, in Humboldthain Park in Gesundbrunnen. Don't be afraid of the bats; they have lived here peacefully for ages. Check the website for details and dates. There is an underground exhibition at the address given, displaying 'Hitler's plans for Berlin' at U-Bahn station Gesundbrunnen, north of Mitte.

↓ ALTERNATIVE BERLIN TOURS

THINGS TO DO

A night at the opera or theatre

staatsoper-berlin.de, deutscheoperberlin.de, berliner-ensemble.de, berlin-buehnen.de, Mitte / Charlottenburg

Berlin has two opera houses, and visiting either is a great experience. The Staatsoper Unter den Linden gives a 50% discount to under 30s, the Deutsche Oper Berlin in Charlottenburg offers a 50% discount for under 21s and 25% discount for students. A night at the opera is quite popular among young people in Berlin – you won't be the only one under thirty. If you are more into theatre, check the Berliner Ensemble, student tickets are 9 euros only.

Ritter Sport Bunte Schokowelt

Franz. Strasse 24, 10117 Mitte, ritter-sport.com

Always wanted to design your own crazy chocolate bar flavour? Milk chocolate with gummy bears – why not? Save up a bit of money and head for the Ritter Sport Colourful Chocolate World, pick your ingredients, and let the people of this chocolate shop make it for you. No, it is not cheap. But yes, it is fun! So sign up for a workshop and make the chocolate bar yourself. Or buy some ready-made flavours; Ritter Sport is a classic choice.

Skatehalle Berlin

Revaler Strasse 99,
10245 Friedrichshain,
skatehalleberlin.com

Do you envy people who can do tricks on their boards? Or even just stay on them? Book yourself a two-hour course at the Skatehalle at R.A.W. Gelände in Friedrichshain. The Good Old Days course on Sunday mornings is for 18+, who at some time rode a board before, and those never even tried. The Weekly-Workday-Workshop (also 18+) is even lower-priced.

StandUpClub

Napelastrasse 18,
12459 Friedrichshain,
standupclub.de

This Club is not related to stand-up comedy but to stand-up paddle. You can explore the city from the water on a SUP board every day from May to September. Or take a tour, short or long, every Sunday during the summer months. No under 16s or non-swimmers allowed.

Stasi Museum

Ruschestrase 103,
10365 Lichtenberg,
stasi-museum.de

The official name of this museum is Forschungs- und Gedenkstätte Normannenstrasse. We could have placed it in the museum section of this book, but this is quite a different experience. You can wander through the rooms of Haus 1, the former Stasi (Ministry of State Security) headquarters during the DDR-era. Erich Mielke, the head of the Stasi, lived and worked here. It's not the most uplifting thing you can do in Berlin, but nonetheless still relevant and important.

FAMOUS PEOPLE

Jerome Boateng

Perhaps one of the most famous and successful football players: Jerome Boateng, born in Berlin in 1988. He played for Hertha BSC, Hamburger SV, Manchester City and Bayern Munich. His brother Kevin-Prince Boateng is a famous football player as well.

David Bowie

He only lived in Berlin for two years during the 70s but fell in love with the city (as we are eager to believe). Bowie recorded three records in the Hansa Studios in Kreuzberg: *Low*, *Heroes* and *Lodger*, known as the Berlin Trilogy. Follow Bowie's footsteps in Berlin and order a drink at his favourite queer cafe Neues Ufer, or have a look at his apartment at Hauptstraße 155 in Schöneberg with a plaque at

the door saying: *We can be heroes, just for one day.*

Marlene Dietrich

Born in 1901 in Schöneberg, Marlene Dietrich was an actress and singer known for her beautiful songs and films, such as *The Blue Angel*, as well as for her status as a fashion icon. During World War II she moved to the US and became a heroine to American soldiers and donated most of her income to refugees. Furthermore, she was known for being openly bisexual and played a lot of androgynous roles in her films. Dietrich died in 1992 in Paris but was buried in Berlin.

Albert Einstein

Born in Germany, the world's most influential scientist moved to Berlin in 1914 but left the country in 1933 never to return. He wanted nothing to do with Nazi Germany. His summer house in the small town of Caputh (a beautiful two-hour bike ride from Brandenburger Tor) is still there and can be visited, but it is also used by 'distinguished thinkers' as a place to get together.

einsteinsommerhaus.de

Nina Hagen

Cool women everywhere in Berlin, but Nina Hagen is probably the most famous, often called the godmother of German punk. Born in 1958, she is still singing. A fun fact: when Angela Merkel left her career as German chancellor, she chose three songs for her leaving do, one of them by Nina Hagen: *Du hast den Farbfilm vergessen*, written in the 70s.

John F. Kennedy

A lot of American presidents came to Berlin and held famous speeches. Not just Obama but also JFK. It is a common misconception that JFK declared himself a pastry in his *Ich bin ein Berliner* speech, held in West-Berlin in 1963 in front of Rathaus Schöneberg. But the grammar *is* correct. A Berliner donut is not referred to as such in German, it is known as a *Krapfchen*. The name Berliner is mainly used in English speaking countries.

Rosa Luxemburg

Rosa was involved in the socialist and revolutionary movement in her birth country Poland as well as Russia and Germany. In order to gain German citizenship, she married a random man whom she left five years later. Rosa contributed to the Marxist theory and wrote the book *The Accumulation of Capital* that criticized imperialism and capitalism. She was 47 when right-wing activists killed her in 1919, but the legacy of this political activist lives on. She has a U-Bahn station, street, and square named after her.

Angela Merkel

Born in Hamburg, raised in Eastern Germany and always politically engaged: Angela Merkel was the very first female chancellor of Germany. She was often considered one of the most powerful women in the world. From 2005-2021 she lived opposite the Museumsinsel, at Am Kupfergraben. Although she might not be everybody's cup of tea, we like the fact that her role model was Marie Curie, the first woman to win a Nobel Prize.

Vladimir Nabokov

From 1922 to 1937 the famous Russian author, best known for *Lolita*, lived in the quiet area of Wilmersdorf. Although Nabokov wrote around nine novels in these years, it is whispered that he never liked the city nor the Germans. A pity. *A Guide to Berlin* (1925) is an interesting short story by his hand.

Iggy Pop

The Godfather of punk, born in the USA, lived in Berlin the same years as David Bowie during the 70s. At the time, both artists were determined to fight their drug addiction. They were close friends, and two great Iggy Pop albums came out of this period in which they worked together: *The Idiot* and *Lust for Life*.

Tom Schilling

Born and raised in Mitte, Schilling never planned to become an actor. But he is now, and his filmography is huge. Among his best-known movies are *A coffee in Berlin (Oh Boy)*, *Fabian – Going to the Dogs*, *Werk ohne Autor (Never Look Away)*. Schilling is not only an actor but also a film producer.

IGGY POP
CHATEAU MARMONT LOS ANGELES 1996

FILMS & SERIES
IN AND ABOUT BERLIN

Lola Rennt, (Run Lola Run, 1998)

In short: a guy loses 100,000 D-Mark which he was supposed to deliver to a criminal on the underground. He has twenty minutes to come up with the money again and asks his girlfriend Lola for help. The movie then unfolds with her taking three different paths. The moral of the story: there are no good or right paths in life, although you could say the right one is the best. One of the coolest films ever made, according to the critics.

Das Leben der Anderen (The Lives of Others, 2006)

Film about a Stasi officer who starts spying on a couple in 1984. The more the officer of the East German secret police listens to them, the more he starts to care and he starts protecting them. We won't tell you how it ends. Beautifully filmed, using a lot of original Stasi equipment.

Oh Boy! (A coffee in Berlin, 2012)

A university drop-out tries to make the best of life and starts wandering the streets of Berlin. A fantastic role by Tom Schilling and we absolutely love the way Berlin is portrayed in this film. Quote: 'Do you know what it's like to have the feeling that all the people around you are honestly kind of weird? But when you think it over, then it becomes clear that the problem is with yourself.'

Babylon Berlin (since 2017)

Staged in Berlin in the 20s and 30s during the Weimar Republic, with a main role for a young police inspector. The 5th season of this series is being made as we write. One of the reasons we watch it is our old school friend Ivo Pietzcker, who plays a part in it.

Victoria (2015)

One city. One night. One take. That's the premise of this film about a girl from Spain who moved to Berlin. She meets a guy, has a flirtation, gets into trouble, and that's where you can't stop watching. It was filmed in various locations in Mitte and Kreuzberg.

Inglourious Basterds (2009)

Filmed in and around Berlin, in places such as Clärchens Ballhaus and Einstein Stammhaus (the original café), this film by Quention Tarantino is a classic about World War II. The 'bastards' are a group of revengeful Jewish soldiers who want to kill Nazi leaders. The cast consists of Brad Pitt, Diane Kruger, and many more American and German actors.

Der Himmel über Berlin (Wings of Desire, 1987)

A beautiful film about two angels living in Berlin, by director Wim Wenders. It is staged in the 80s, right before the Wall came down. One of the angels falls in love with a human, a trapeze artist from the local circus, and wants to become human too. The movie is filmed mainly in former West Berlin and shot in both black and white and colour. A classic.

Good Bye, Lenin! (2003)

What to do if your mother is a firm and highly respected communist, and has been in a coma for a long time during which the Wall came down? You make her believe nothing has happened and the DDR still exists. A very funny, witty watch, with lots of DDR nostalgia.

Sonnenallee (1999)

Thomas Brussig (see page 86) wrote not only the book but also adapted it into the screenplay for this film. Sonnenalleen is a street that was once divided by the Berlin Wall. The film is all about life on the 'wrong' side of history. The film was both seen as DDR criticism and despised as being too romantic about DDR life. Judge the movie for yourself.

Dogs of Berlin (2018)

Take two policemen who have little in common, the Berlin underworld, a battle for power, and corruption, put them in a blender and ta-daaa: a very successful tv series. For those with *Fernweh* or looking forward to seeing Berlin, the series was shot primarily in the city.

Captain America: Civil War (2016)

For all Marvel fans: a few scenes of *Captain America: Civil War* were filmed in Berlin. End of story. There may be many reasons to watch a Marvel movie, and this is yours.

Druck (Shame, since 2018)

The Norwegian show *Skam* became so popular that it's been remade in multiple different countries, including the German edition: *Druck* (meaning pressure). The show centres around a group of highschool friends, and explores themes in their everyday lives: friendship, love, identity, school, relationships, sexuality, et cetera ... Each season is dedicated to a new character, and with *Druck*'s eight seasons there's something in it for everyone. What's special about any version of the series is that they try to make the characters seem as real as possible, creating realistic Instagram accounts for characters, giving little updates on YouTube, as well as more content you can only find if you look for it. *Druck* takes place in Berlin, and it's very telling about everyday teenagers in the city.

BOOKS IN & ABOUT BERLIN

Am kurzeren Ende der Sonnenallee (The short end of the Sonnenallee) – Thomas Brussig

Brussig writes, with a lot of humor, about his life in former East Berlin where he was born in 1964. Two of his books were translated into English, both are page-turners. *The short end of the Sonnenallee* is about the daily life of a group of young people living in the DDR during the Cold War. It's a pity that not all Brussig's books are translated into English ... Time to improve your German!

Berlin Alexanderplatz – Alfred Döblin

A 1929 novel, a classic and an absolute must-read if you want to understand how life in Berlin was over a hundred years ago. If you enjoy the book, also pick up Döblin's short novel *Two women and a poisoning*, based on a true story that took place in the same period.

Wir Kinder vom Bahnhof Zoo (Zoo Station) – Christiane F.

A classic among students: this book about (and told by) a young drug addict, a teenager living on the streets of Berlin near Bahnhof Zoo. Besides the addiction, the book is also about things in life we all experience. The original title of the book is *Wir Kinder Vom Bahnhof Zoo* and was first published in 1978.

Other People's Clothes – Calla Henkel

This novel follows an art student from America as she goes to study abroad in Berlin hoping to escape the pain of her best friend's murder. After her and a fellow student find an apartment to rent, they start suspecting that their

landlady might be stalking them. As it turns out, she is, and she's writing her next thriller about the two students. This is truly a book for people looking for more complicated, 'unhinged', female characters.

The Berlin Stories – Christopher Isherwood

Is it a coincidence that so many books take place in the 1930s? Isherwood set his beautiful book *The Berlin Stories* in that time. His book *Goodbye to Berlin* also deserves some hours of reading. We love the stories, the humour, and Christopher Isherwood's beautiful writing.

Emil und die Detektive (Emil and the Detectives) – Erich Kästner

A children's book, probably read by all German kids. As children's books can be very comforting at times, why not re-read it? Emil is a twelve-year-old who gets robbed on the train to Berlin, where he meets a local gang of children known as 'the detectives'. All ends well, evidently. The book has been adapted into several films.

Das kunstseidene Mädchen (The artificial silk girl) – Irmgard Keun

If you enjoyed Christopher Isherwood, you should pick up this book too. It's about the 1930s in Berlin as well but written from a female perspective. The author was censored by the Nazis and the book disappeared for some time but was republished in the 1970s.

Austerlitz – W.G. Sebald

The protagonist of this novel, Berlin born Jacques Austerlitz, lives in Antwerp. His mother died during the Holocaust, and he becomes obsessed with her past. Throughout the novel, Austerlitz visits Berlin in search of clues about her life and what became of her during the war. The vivid descriptions of Berlin's streets and buildings provide a backdrop to Austerlitz's story, giving an insight into the city's history and the enduring impact of World War II.

Babylon Berlin – Volker Kutscher

'It's 1929 and Berlin is the vibrating metropolis of post-war Germany – full of bars and brothels and dissatisfied workers at the point of revolt.' Do you need more encouragement to read this book? It's a beautifully told tale about the difficulties of living in the early 20th century. It's also been published as a graphic novel, and see page 83 for the popular TV series adaptation.

The Innocent – Ian McEwan

One of McEwan's best novels is set in Berlin during the 1950s. A 25-year-old Englishman becomes involved in Operation Gold, a cooperation of the American and British secret services CIA and MI6. An exciting story about spies and the Cold War as well as a love story.

The Gift – Vladimir Nabokov

Nabokov's last book, written between 1935 and 1937, is about a Russian writer living in Berlin. It reads as two books in one: the one you're reading and the one the protagonist wants to write. Nabokov fans often regard this book as his best.

Herr Lehmann (Berlin Blues) – Sven Regener

The book's protagonist, Herr Lehmann, lives a hedonistic life in Kreuzberg and is avoiding all responsibilities in life. It's 1989 and his life is good. Until it isn't. You'll get a nice look into the 80s and life in Berlin at the time, and it's a funny book.

The Girl in Berlin – Elizabeth Wilson

'Trust no one.' A not-so-comforting theme for a book, but this novel is all about spying and secrets. The story is set during the Cold War and partly takes place in London.

FUN FACTS

Bananensprayer

Have you spotted spray-painted bananas in the streets? They are made by Thomas Baumgärtel, an artist from Cologne who calls himself Bananensprayer. The banana is sprayed next to every gallery he holds in high esteem. Look out for them on Auguststrasse in Mitte, and on Potsdamer Strasse.

bananensprayer.de

Confusing house numbers

In the former eastern part of the city the house numbers can be quite confusing. Usually, all the even numbers in a street are on one side, and the odd on the other. Not true in some streets in Prenzlauer Berg, where the numbering goes from 1-2-3 an so forth on one side. At the end of the street, the numbering continues on the other side, with the lowest and the highest house numbers on opposite ends.

Currywurst

Eaten with or without *Pommes* (chips) this is one of the most eaten snacks in Berlin. The *Currywurst* was allegedly invented in 1949 by Berlin housewife Hertha Heuwer. When meeting an English soldier, she exchanged spirits for ketchup, curry powder, and Worcestershire sauce – ingredients all proper Englishmen seem to always have at hand. She accidentally mixed the ingredients and decided to pour them over a sausage: a culinary mistake that turned out the recipe of a lifetime. Hertha patented her sauce, and the rest is history.

Fernweh

German is not typically considered a subtle language – you can find a funny video online about the difference between the pronunciations of *Schmetterling* as opposed to the French *papillon*. They both mean butterfly but the sounds are vastly different. But some German words are just beautiful. We love *Wackelpudding*, also known as *Götterspeise* (our love goes to the word for jelly, not so much the dessert itself). Other words to learn by heart, just for the fun of it and also because they're almost

untranslatable: *Kuddelmuddel* (a chaotic situation), the well-known word *Wanderlust* (the desire to leave your home and travel the world), *Schnapsidee* (ideas that only come up when drunk), *Fernweh* (longing for distant places) and *Waldeinsamkeit* (feeling happy when you are alone in the woods). Two German words that connect to your trip to Berlin are *Reisefieber* (travel fever) and *Vorfreude* (joyful anticipation).

Flaschensammler

Under many street bins, you will find a bottle crate to put your empty beer or soda bottles with *Pfand* (deposit) in. These bottles will be taken by *Flaschensammler* (bottle collectors), who will earn some money from returning the bottles to Spätis or the supermarket. Many bottle collectors are homeless people, who can earn a lot of euros without having to empty the street bins. If you find yourself finishing your Club-Mate, place the bottle under the waste bins rather than inside them. Look out for the funny sentences on the bins: they are all different.

Greenest city of Europe

You'll notice many small parks in areas such as Prenzlauer Berg and Kreuzberg. Berlin is in fact the greenest city in Europe. It has many small parks, green spaces, parks, and even forests and gardens. There is always a park nearby – big or small – for a quick picnic or a little rest under the trees. Dog owners know this too: more than 200,000 dogs live in Berlin, and they must be the happiest dogs in the world.

Nine times bigger

Since Brexit, Berlin is the EU's most populous city. Berlin has about 3.8 million inhabitants whereas Paris for example has

2.2 million citizens. But Berlin is actually nine time larger than Paris; Berlin's total land area is 891 km2 while Paris covers 105 km2. While the city centres are similar in size, Berlin has a lot of green parks, forests, surrounding its centre.

Rainy days vs museums

Sometimes the rain can last for days in Berlin. But the city has more museums than rainy days: there are about 105 rainy day vs roughly 190 museums. So whenever it starts to pour, head for the nearest museum. You'll probably end up somewhere new every time it starts to rain.

museumsportal-berlin.de

Streetlights

Since 1989, Berlin is no longer divided into East and West. But still, after all these years, the division can be seen from the sky at night. Streetlights in the former East emit orange light, while those in the former West are bright and white. The city still uses different lamps and fittings, which means this beautiful image from outer space will continue to exist.

That pipe again

All over town, you can see overhead blue and pink pipes. The pipes even have their own hashtag #thatpipeagain on Instagram. Berlin always has a *Baustelle* (construction site) somewhere, with new buildings being built. From the sites, the groundwater is pumped up and transported to the Spree River through pink or blue pipes. Mystery solved.

PHOTO SPOTS

Photoautomat

photoautomat.de

Photos are generally taken best in the early morning or late afternoon. We suggest you visit at least one of the photo spots below. But first things first: don't forget to go to one of the Photoautomat (photo booth) on the streets. You will find them anywhere: in parks, on markets, indoors, randomly placed all over Berlin. There are roughly thirty Photoautomats in Berlin, mainly in Mitte, Kreuzberg, and Friedrichshain. You will need some change to operate them.

**Fernsehturm &
Park Inn Hotel**

*Panoramastrasse 1a,
10178 Mitte, tv-turm.de*

Treat yourself to a ticket and go up the famous TV tower. On a bright day, the view over the city is spectacular. The only thing you won't see is the beloved tower itself. Perhaps even better (or at least much cheaper) is the top floor of the nearby Park Inn Hotel. You'll get the best view of the tower itself. Tickets for the rooftop can be bought at the reception desk.

Urania Weltzeituhr

*Alexanderplatz 1, 10178
Mitte, weltzeituhr-berlin.
de*

One of our favourites in the city: the *Weltzeituhr*, or the World Clock, that was built in 1968-1969. The round statue shows the names of 146 cities around the world, all with their different time zones. Make sure to stop by when it's relatively quiet in the early morning.

Siegessäule

Grosser Stern, 10557
Mitte / Tiergarten

The 67 metre tall *Sieggessäule* (Victory Column) is an imposing column topped with a golden sculpture in the middle of Tiergarten Park. Barack Obama once held a speech at its foot, drawing a crowd of around 200,000. The statue glows nicely on a sunny day. Climb the 285 steps for a view over the city.

Oberbaumbrücke

Mühlenstrasse, 10234
Friedrichshain

Unless you prefer modern architecture, the Oberbaumbrücke with its two small towers is arguably the most beautiful bridge of Berlin. It was built in 1896 and connects the areas Friedrichshain and Kreuzberg. Take the U-Bahn to Warschauer Strasse and walk towards the bridge. For the best picture, wait for the yellow S-Bahn to pass: the brown bricks form a nice contrast with the yellow carriages.

Viktoriapark

Katzbachstrasse, 10965
Kreuzberg

A waterfall in the middle of the city? *Aber natürlich!* The quiet Viktoriapark between Kreuzberg and Friedrichshain is located on one of the highest points of the city. Don't leave Berlin without a photo of those waterfalls.

Park Tempelhofer Feld

Oderstrasse/
Herrfurthstrasse, 12049
Neukölln

Rent a bike and head for Tempelhofer Feld to take pictures of an abandoned airport (closed in 2008). Ride a few rounds on its former runways, enjoy the silence ... ever been to an airport without any noise? You can book a tour through the massive building of Tempelhof itself.

Teufelsberg

*Teufelsseechaussee
10, 14193 Grunewald,
teufelsberg-berlin.de*

Built on the rubble of World War II, Teufelsberg is one of the highest places in Berlin. It housed an American listening station during the Cold War. Nowadays it's abandoned and perfect for photo shoots, as well learning everything about the DDR-era and the Cold War if you book a tour. The view over the city is an added bonus. Take the S-Bahn S7 to Heerstrasse or Grunewald. Entrance 5 euros, with or without a guided tour.

↓ TEMPELHOFER FELD

FOOD AND DRINKS

BREAKFAST, BRUNCH & COFFEE

44 Brekkie

Named after the house
number of their first location
on Rykstrasse 44, this little
Berlin chain of breakfast
and brunch restaurants is
super popular. You'll find the
restaurants in Prenzlauer Berg,
Friedrichshain, and Kreuzberg.

44brekkie.com or insta @brekkie44

The Barn

The Barn started as a very
small shop in Mitte, but this
coffee chain is slowly taking
over Berlin. They currently
are on ten locations in Mitte
as well as Charlottenburg,
Neukölln, and Prenzlauer
Berg. Their light roasted coffee
comes from farms all over the
world, and they serve good
cakes and sandwiches.

thebarn.de

Café Datscha

A *Datscha*, or summer house in the countryside, is an eastern tradition. The breakfast at Datscha is classic and modern at the same time. Treat yourself to a large breakfast at one of their three locations (Mitte, Friedrichshain and Kreuzberg), vegan or omnivore. We love the *Weekend zu zweit* (weekend for two): a huge breakfast that will keep you going for quite some time for under thirty euros.

datscha.de

What do you fancy, love?

You can find our favourite bagels in the city in Mitte and Charlottenburg and you should have a stop at one of their shops. They also offer the biggest array of drinks: juices, smoothies, superfood shakes, coffee, tea, you can find just about anything here. If you don't fancy a bagel, have a sandwich, pastry, cake, or muesli bowl.

whatdoyoufancylove.de

Zeit für Brot

Ah yes, the famous *Zimtschnecke* or cinnamon roll. It's huge, so if you're not into large breakfasts you might want to share. The Zeit für Brot bakeries are known for their sweet pastries, but don't forget to try their breads. Five locations: Mitte, Prenzlauer Berg, Schöneberg, and Wilmersdorf.

zeitfuerbrot.com

Cafe Buondi

In a street just outside of bustling Mitte you'll find Cafe Buondi, a sunny cafe with amazing breakfast and lunch options. Unfortunately, they don't offer many vegetarian and vegan options, so be sure to check the menu beforehand.

Eichendorffstrasse 6, 10115 Mitte, buondibreakfastbar.com

Father Carpenter

Located in a courtyard right in the middle of Berlin is Father Carpenter, known for their delicious brunch menu and specialty coffees. They don't take bookings and, on some days, especially when the sun is out, it can get really busy and there might be a queue. But we feel it is definitely worth the wait.

Münzstrasse 21, 10178 Mitte, fathercarpenter.com

Keyser Soze

Every day from 8am to 3.30pm you can have a nice breakfast at Keyser Soze, a lovely corner bar. When the weather is good, seat yourself on the benches against the window. The *Strammer Max* is a classic German dish they serve: two fried eggs with ham and dark bread. It's also a good spot if you're craving a fruit salad or something veggie.

Tucholskystrasse 33, 10117 Mitte, keyser-soze.de

Nah am Wasser

Egg lovers: this is your place. Start your day in Berlin with all sorts of scrambled eggs, omelettes, or the typical *Eier im Glas* (soft-boiled eggs in a glass). They serve many other breakfast and lunch dishes.

Kiehlufer 55, 12059 Neukölln, nahamwasser.de

BIERGÄRTEN (BEER GARDENS)

Café am Neuen See

Drinking beer while overlooking a lake, without leaving the city? If that's your idea of a good time, head for Tiergarten Park where this beer garden is located. The *Brezeln* and *Leberkäse* (very Bavarian), pizza, and other food are great companions to their beers. You could rent a little rowing boat and explore the lake, but honestly, getting another round of beer is cheaper.

Liechtensteinallee 2, 10787 Mitte / Tiergarten, cafeamneuensee.de

Schleusenkrug

A charming beer garden that serves a late breakfast? Yes, please! That breakfast could be chili con carne. This beer garden is not as well-known, but it can still get crowded on hot days. It is located north of the Zoo, at the end of Tiergarten Park. It is best reached by bike, or from S-Bahn station Tiergarten.

Müller-Breslau-Strasse 14b, 10623 Mitte / Tiergarten, schleusenkrug.de

Prater

One of our favourite beer gardens. Apart from a long winter break, it's open most of the year, Tuesdays to Saturdays. Bikes can be parked right behind the entrance and after that, you'll see nothing but large trees, a vast number of wooden tables, and benches that can seat around 600 people, and yeah, a lot of beer. Inside the garden you'll also find a Gaststätte for the perfect *Schnitzel*, but you can also order sausages or corn on the cob from the little stands next to the beer stands.

Kastanienallee 7-9, 10435 Prenzlauer Berg, prater-biergarten.de

Golgatha

This beer garden has been here since forever, or 1928 to be precise. At that time, it was called Terrassen am Kreuzberg but they changed their name to Golgatha in 1977. Find yourself right in the middle of Viktoriapark, a nice green area close-ish to the Bergmannkiez and Tempelhofer Park. There are not that many tourists, but a lot of locals find their way to this cosy beer garden.

Katzbachstrasse (Viktoriapark), 10965 Kreuzberg, golgatha-berlin.de

↓ PRATER

FOOD AND DRINKS

Klunkerkranich

A beer garden disguised as a rooftop bar. Quite popular, you might have to queue to get in, but the trick is to be early (they open around 4pm) and give yourself some time to find the entrance as well. Klunkerkranich calls itself 'a cultural rooftop garden' and it's a perfect place for chilling and overlooking the city.

Karl-Marx-Strasse 66, 12043 Neukölln, klunkerkranich.org

STREET FOOD & SNACKS

Shiso Burger

Japanese hamburgers may sound a bit odd, but nevertheless, the burgers taste great! The extremely popular Shiso Burger started as a small place in Auguststrasse (Mitte) but can now be found at two other Berlin locations – and is opening restaurants across the globe. From the Chili Lemon Burger to the Veggie Burger, everything from its small menu tastes good.

shisoburger.com

Yarok

Your chance to try Syrian food! You'll find just a few benches inside and outside. We can recommend the tabouleh salad, the full salad (fava beans with chickpeas) and even the plain pita bread is yummy. Sufficient vegetarian options as well.

Torstrasse 195, 10115 Mitte, yarok-restaurant.de

Konnopke's

East-West rivalry in *Currywurst* country: Konnopke's Imbiss, under the S-Bahn and close to U-Bahn station Eberswalder Strasse is the iconic *Currywurst* stand in the former East. Opt for the classic *Currywurst* (there's a vegan *Wurst* too) or have *Kartoffelsalat* (potato salad) with it. Closed on Sundays and Mondays.

Schönhauser Allle 44b, 10435 Prenzlauer Berg, konnopke-imbiss.de

Dolores

'Your California Amigo 2x in Berlin'. The colourful restaurants of Dolores (Mitte and Schöneberg) have the best burritos around, and we tried many. Choose one from the menu or create your own. Not that into burritos? Order a bowl for about the same price – somewhere between 8 and 11 euros.

dolores-burritos.de

Mustafa's Gemüse Kebap

Of course, there are more good kebabs (in German often written as *Kebap*) to be found in Berlin, but part of the fun of eating one here is the queue. We're not kidding, it's long and the wait is up to 45 minutes. We might not be the only

travel guide mentioning this little stand. Don't let the name fool you, you can order a *döner* with chicken as well as a veggie one. It is well worth the wait, we promise.

Mehringdamm 62, 10961 Kreuzberg, mustafas.de

Markthalle Neun

A market hall in Kreuzberg filled with street food. Quite an ordinary food hall with shops in some respects, but we love Markthalle Neun for stalls like Heisser Hobel for *Käsespätzle* (egg noodles with cheese), barbecue at Big Stuff, dim sum at the Bao Gao Club, and Chao She for more Chinese food. Stalls come and go. The Markthalle is open daily but best visited on weekends.

Eisenbahnstrasse 42-43, 10997 Kreuzberg, markthalleneun.de

Mehlspeisen & Kuchen
* Kaiserschmarrn
* Marillentopfenknödl
* Sachertorte
* Olgas Käsekuchen
♡
Eiskaffee, Eisschokolade
♡
Aperol
* Keine

Burgermeister

Located in a former public toilet under a bridge, with the S-Bahn passing by every other minute. It might not sound like an attractive place to be having a burger. But you should. Because (1) this must be one of the most unexpected street food locations on earth, and (2) they simply make the best burgers. The latter resulted in thirteen more Burgermeister in Berlin, and they don't seem intent to stop expanding just yet.

Oberbaumstrasse 8, 10997 Kreuzberg, burgermeister.com

Curry 36

Oh boy, are we really going for *Currywurst*? Well, yes, we are! You must try it at least once in your life. Unless you're a veggie of ... nope, not a good excuse either, as Curry 36 serves a vegan currywurst, or – it's Berlin after all – you can have an organic *Wurst*. Tom Hanks' favourite in Berlin, allegedly, has four outlets in town, with the OG since 1980 on Mehringdamm.

Mehringdamm 36, 10961 Kreuzberg, curry36.de

KAFFEE & KUCHEN

Café Anna Blume & SowohlAlsAuch

To have a classic German afternoon, indulge in a slice of cake at this flower-filled café in the Kollwitzkiez. Do you come at a time when there are no tables left? Just hop across the street to SowohlAlsAuch, another excellent cake spot.

Kollwitzstrasse 83, cafe-anna-blume.de / Kollwitzstrasse 88, 10435 Prenzlauer Berg, sowohlalsauch.berlin

Jubel

Meaning 'cheering' in German, at Jubel little sweet creations are made. To be eaten right there, with a good coffee, tea, or juice. There is only room for fourteen people. Every single bite is worth its price. Closed on Mondays and Tuesdays.

Hufelandstrasse 10, 10407 Prenzlauer Berg, jubel.berlin

Kauf dich Glücklich

This German fashion chain has one shop where they also sell *The Best Waffles* and *Das Leckerste Eis*. Get hold of a seat on the terrace overlooking one of the nicest streets in the area and go for that waffle. In summer with strawberries, in winter with chocolate.

Oderbergerstrasse 44, 10435 Prenzlauer Berg, kaufdichglueclich-shop.de

Katie's Blue Cat

Sweet little spot in the heart of Kreuzkölln that serves English and American sweets. It's a place that always smells good, where the coffee is great, and with a terrace to linger on.

Friedelstrasse 31, 12047 Kreuzberg, katiesbluecat.de

Albatross Bakery

The bakery sells fantastic bread but also created inventions like Pistachio Ricotta Croissants. It sells these alongside a variety of other filled croissants, hot buns, *tarte tatin*, and more.

Graefestrasse 66-67, 10967 Kreuzberg, albatrossberlin.com

DINNER

Mmaah

Korean galore! What started as a little shop close to Tempelhofer Feld, is now a chain with eight locations dotted throughout the city. Mmaah Korean BBQ Express is all about sizzling chicken, rice, and vegetables. We love their vegetarian options too. This is a great stop before a night out on the town.

mmaah.de, insta @mmaah_bbq

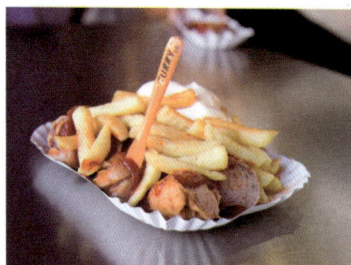

Transit

Thai and tapas might sound like a strange combination, but it is in fact quite delicious. Order a few dishes from the short menu, and if you're still hungry afterwards, simply order more. There are three different locations: in Mitte, Kreuzberg, and Friedrichshain.

transit-restaurants.com

Standard Serious Pizza

They started with a branch in Prenzlauer Berg but now Standard Serious Pizza can also be found in Mitte and Charlottenburg. This is the best Neapolitan style pizza in town. Allegedly, it is even the best pizza outside Italy, but do try for yourself. The atmosphere is nice too.

standard-berlin.de

Zola

If you like your pizza a little bit funkier than the ordinary margherita, go to Zola. And don't check their Instagram if you're hungry. There are four locations in Berlin, the two in Kreuzberg are the most centrally located.

insta @zola_berlin

Monsieur Vuong

Some restaurants always have a queue on their doorstep. At Vietnamese restaurant Monsieur Vuong, this has been the case ever since the day they opened. It's no wonder. The food is delicious as well as affordable and the wooden tables on the pavement are great for some people watching. The menu changes twice a week.

Alte Schönhauser Strasse 46, 10119 Mitte, monsieurvuong.de

Strandbad Mitte

Next to ice cream parlour Spoonful you'll find Strandbad Mitte. Although strand means beach, there is no water or sand in sight. But the atmosphere is very relaxed, and they serve great main courses for under twenty euros. Special occasion? Go for the three-course menu. The small side street off Auguststrasse is a dead-end, so don't try to find Strandbad from the side of the football pitch.

Kleine Hamburger Strasse 16, 10117 Mitte, insta @strandbadmitte

Yam Yam

In the mood for Korean food? Head to Yam Yam, known for their kimchi. Try the sizzling bowl of bibimbap: rice, a lot of veggies, and a fried egg to top it off. It can be ordered with meat or as a vegan meal. It can get a bit crowded, so it works to come a bit later for lunch, or to make a reservation.

Alte Schönhauser Strasse, 10119 Mitte, yamyam-berlin.de

Purgal

This beautiful delicatessen, not far from Rosenthaler Platz, has a few seats both inside and out. In the open plan kitchen, they prepare delicious sandwiches and small dishes. In the deli you'll find all sorts of nice goodies, including tasty cakes. It only opens on Saturdays and Sundays.

Brunnenstrasse 162, 10119 Mitte, purgaldelicatessen.de

Knödelwirtschaft

Knödel, or dumplings, are famous in Südtirol. This is where the owner of these two restaurants was born. Most dumplings contain meat, although there are vegetarian options too. Make sure not to leave without sampling the *Griessknödel*, sweet dessert dumplings. Add Schnapps to wash them down.

Stargarder Strasse 3, 10437 Prenzlauer Berg /
Fuldastrasse 33, 12045 Neukölln,
knoedelwirtschaft.de

Oderbergerstrasse

Other than a few good vintage shops dotted around, the entire Oderbergerstrasse basically consists of one long line of restaurants. You can opt for Indian at Naan, Vietnamese at Vietnam Village, shared dining at MaMi, and yes, classical German cuisine at Oderquelle or Kiezkantine. Just stroll along the many options and take your pick. It's all up to you.

Oderbergerstrasse, 10435 Prenzlauer Berg

An einem Sonntag im August

They have a very short menu, but it contains just what you need after a long day in the city: chili con or sin carne, Thai curry bowl, or goulash soup. They serve bar snacks and salads too.

Kastanienallee 103, 10435 Prenzlauer Berg,
an-einem-sonntag-im-august.de

Osmans Töchter

You can have Turkish food anywhere in Berlin, but it's often not quite like this: they serve their selection of hot and cold mezze in a nicely decorated restaurant with a lovely ambiance. It is run by two sisters, hence the name of the place (*Töchter* means daughters).

Pappelallee 15, 10437 Prenzlauer Berg,
osmanstoechter.de

Sabor a mí

If you've visited Markthalle IX on a Thursday, you've probably seen this taco booth. But they own a restaurant too, which is open Wednesdays to Sundays. Tacos galore! They also offer huge servings of guacamole, quesadillas, tostadas, and soups. Authentic Mexican comfort food, lovingly prepared by a lovely family.

Grünbergerstrasse 83, 10245 Friedrichshain

Café Mugrabi

This beautiful little café opposite Görlitzer Park is perfect for lunch or an early dinner (they close at 6pm). It is quite easy to find favourites such as hummus or shakshuka on the Israelian menu, but we recommend the sabich roll and caulilflower too. Vegetarians will also be happy.

Görlitzer Strasse 58, 10997 Kreuzberg, cafemugrabi.com

Nest

Nest is a bustling place with an international menu with a Berlin twist. A bit of German influences mixed with a lot of Mediterranean, Caribbean, and Persian cuisines. Go to Nest for breakfast, brunch, lunch or dinner. Open Thursdays to Sundays.

Görlitzerstrasse 52, 10997 Kreuzberg, cafenest.de

Max und Moritz

Max und Moritz has been going strong since 1902. Traditional German favourites like *Kutscher Gulash*, *Berliner Kartoffelsuppe* and *Königsberger Klopse* are served in classic stube-like surroundings. Check the extensive menu on their website. Cash only!

Oranienstrasse 162, 10969 Kreuzberg, maxundmoritzberlin.de

Kimchi Princess

Great Korean food in a hip environment. The menu includes the famous Korean barbecue, with a vegan version available too. Or you could opt for classics like Bibimbap, crispy chicken or a tofu salad. You will certainly have a great night out.

Skalitzer Strasse 36, 10999 Kreuzberg, kimchiprincess.com

Kauz & Kiebitz

Kauz & Kiebitz, offer 'craft beer, booze & comfort food'. Well, what more do you need? They have twelve draught beers on tap, and they serve a rotating selection of bar food. In the back of the pub, you'll find cocktailbar Truffle Pig.

Reuterstrasse 47, 12047 Neukölln, kauzundkiebitz.de

BRLO Brwhouse

Close to Park am Gleisdreieck, you'll find this craft beer brewery. It is housed in a building constructed of almost forty sea containers. Aside from the obvious beer drinking, shared dining is popular at BRLO Brwhouse.

Schöneberger Strasse 16, 10963 Schöneberg, brlo.de

BRING THE PARENTS

Cookies Cream

Nine out of ten times a fantastic Michelin-rated restaurant caters to omnivores. Not this one; it's heaven for vegetarians. Take someone with a big wallet and prepare for the dinner of a lifetime. Cookies Cream is located at Crackers, another one for your foodie bucket list.

Behrenstrasse 55, 10117 Mitte, cookiescream.com

Jolesch

Maybe not even the most expensive restaurant in town, but somehow it feels like you should eat here with your parents or grandparents. The vibe at this place is both old-fashioned and modern. They serve the best *Schnitzel* in town – even a vegetarian one. When in doubt, order all the sides. For dessert you must try the *Marillenknödel*.

Muskauer Strasse 1, 10997 Kreuzberg, jolesch.de

Paris Bar

The classic in the former West, founded in 1950. This bar was frequented by David Bowie and many, many other artists. The food is, evidently, French, but the real draw of Paris Bar is the atmosphere, which you just want to soak up.

Kantstrasse 152, 10623 Charlottenburg, parisbar.net

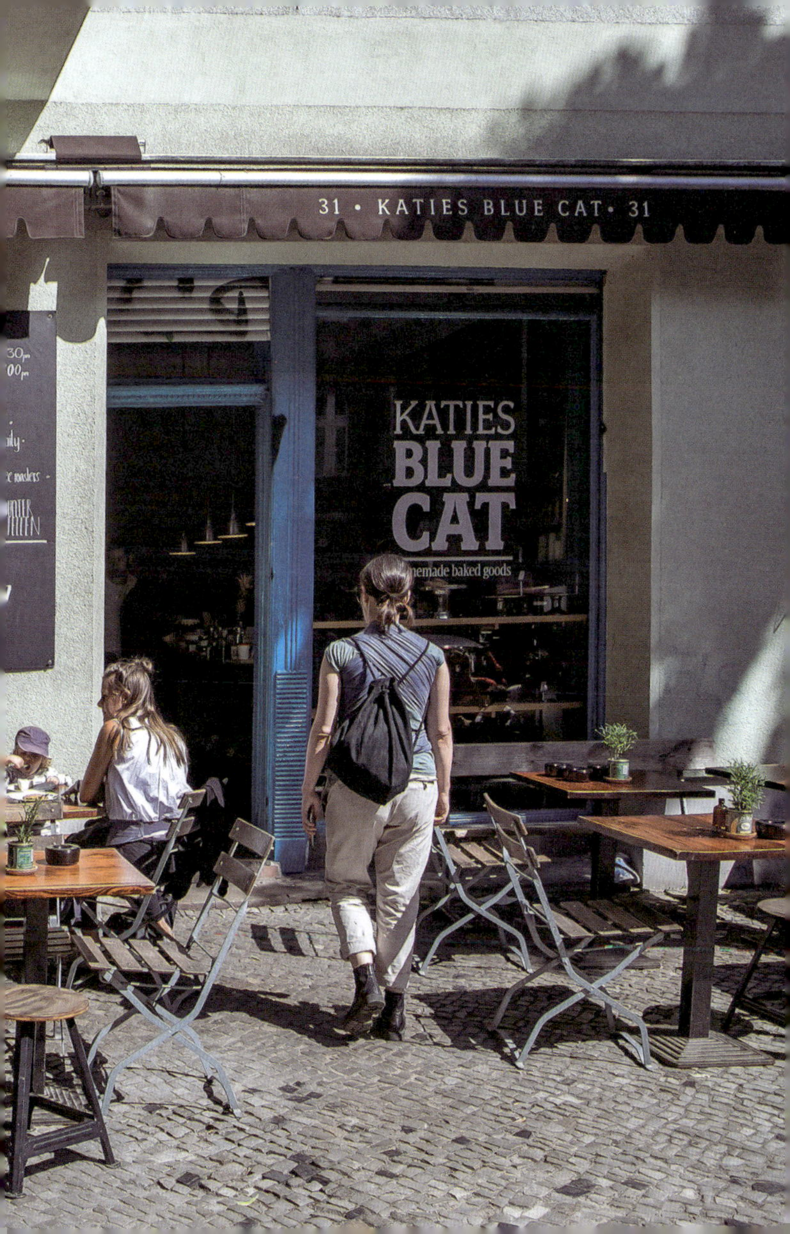
31 • KATIES BLUE CAT• 31
KATIES
BLUE
CAT
nemade baked goods

GOING OUT

SPÄTIS, KNEIPEN & CLUBS

SPÄTIS

It is important to note that in Germany – and specifically Berlin – the drinking culture revolves around the *Späti* (short for *Spätverkauf*, meaning late sale). Drinking at Spätis or buying drinks at Spätis before taking them to one of the parks or lakes that dot the Berlin urban landscape, is one of the locals' most popular activities. It is not only more budget friendly than drinking at a bar, it also encourages you to not sit still in a single location but wander from Späti to Späti, and from park to park. Most Berliners will opt for the Sternburg Pils (colloquially known as *Sterni*), as it is often the cheapest option.

Rosenthaler Kiosk

Located at the bustling Rosenthaler Platz in the heart of Berlin, this Späti is right next to the scenic Weinbergspark. You can choose between grabbing a seat at one of their outside beer benches or wandering to the park and sit at the central pond to enjoy your drinks there. Should you feel a little peckish after a drink or two, the famous Rosenthaler Grill just across the street offers one of the best Döner Kebabs in the area.

Rosenthaler Strasse 50, 13127 Mitte

KNEIPEN

Schokoladen

Schokoladen e.V. is a last bastion of old Berlin, standing in all its dilapidated glory right at the heart of the ever-modernising Mitte area. As the name suggests, the building that houses this unique Bar was formerly a chocolate factory. It now boasts a new kind of treat: live concerts, karaoke nights, and cheap drinks. Concerts range from reggae and power pop to punk, rock, and ska, and feature many up-and-coming local bands. These are usually followed by DJ sets that go late into the night. Schokoladen truly is the perfect place to catch a show, have a beer and play a round of *Kicker* or foosball.

Ackerstrasse 169, 10115 Mitte,
schokoladen-mitte.de

Eschschloraque

Opened in 1995, this bar is one of the oldest standing bars in Mitte, as well as one of its best kept secrets. Eschschloraque is about as strange as its name. Characterised by its dark and smoky interior, filled with various metallic art pieces and sculptures, this bar is a great destination all year round. In winter, the bar's large and cosy interior offers shelter from the often harsh and dark Berlin cold, and brightens your spirits with DJs, dance performances, and well ... spirits. In summer, the bar has a huge cocktail garden and outside bar where a visceral vibrancy of chatter, laughter, and the clinking of glasses takes form, inviting you to stay in this artistic oasis. Or perhaps explore the other institutions in the same courtyard: Kino Central, The Monster Kabinett, and Neurotitan. Photography is strictly forbidden both indoors and outside.

Rosenthalerstrasse 39, 10178 Mitte,
eschschloraque.de

Meine Bar ICI

This bar feels more as though it belongs in some side street in a small Italian town, and yet there it is. On the quiet but charming Auguststrasse, a dark, wooden façade beckons you in. The extremely narrow and long interior is lit almost entirely by candlelight, and the walls are brimming with black and white photos, empty frames, and crucifixes. In the summer, they open their extended terrace, seating you out on the street. In winter, the bar is usually jam packed, smoke-filled, and home to the pleasant din of scattered conversation. Meine Bar ICI is home to a slightly older crowd. Unlike some other bars, the music isn't very loud and the atmosphere more conducive to a good long conversation rather than a dance party.

Auguststrasse 61, 10117 Mitte

Hackbarth's

Opened shortly after the fall of the Berlin Wall, Hackbarth's has quickly established itself as an institution in Mitte's nightlife. Its interior is modelled after a ship at sea. The triangular bronze bar represents the bow, and the blue and gold wallpaper evokes a sunrise over a blue sea. Especially in summer, this is the perfect place to get an Aperol Spritz and enjoy a dreamy sunset. Additionally, for those not too keen on second-hand smoke, Hackbarth's recently became a non-smoking bar.

Auguststrasse 49a, 10119 Mitte

Z Bar

On a quiet side street of an otherwise busy neighbourhood, small but cosy Z Bar offers a great selection of wines and beers. They play an eclectic mix of music, and they host film screenings and the occasional intimate concert in their back room.

Bergstrasse 2, 10115 Mitte, zbarberlin.com

Cafe Morgenrot

A grounded leftist cafe and bar, Morgenrot offers a great selection of hot and cold drinks, as well as bar snacks. In winter, they open their basement for table tennis nights where heated matches take place. Or you can enjoy a light-hearted game of *Around the world*, a great way to meet new people. A Sterni (Sternenburg Pils) is still just €2.50, making it one of the cheapest beers in the area.

Kastanienallee 85, 10435 Prenzlauer Berg, cafe-morgenrot.de

Trauerspiel

A real Berliner *Eckkneipe* (literally a corner bar, but here it is meant as a bar for locals), Trauerspiel is a true hidden gem. With its totally unique interior and bar layout, this bar is perfect for a night out, by yourself or with others. Their selection of local beers is interesting and ever-changing. The Mexikaner is phenomenal, especially with a little added Tobasco. You can get lost looking at the portraits of Schlager singers and political figures that bespeckle the green curtained walls.

Milastrasse 7, 10437 Prenzlauer Berg

Baiz

A punk bar through and through, Baiz is a real pillar of the local community and art scene. This candlelit Bar on Schönhauser Allee serves affordable drinks alongside a great programme of poetry readings, community events, fundraisers, and political lectures. You can also pick up a copy of *Stressfaktor*, a monthly zine with an expansive programme of that month's concerts, exhibitions, and protests.

Schönhauser Allee 26a, 10435 Prenzlauer Berg, baiz.info

8MM

Cornerstone of the Berlin alternative music scene: 8MM has hosted a wild array of music acts, spanning from obscure local oddities to international rockstars such as the Brian Jonestown Massacre. The drinks are affordable, and the DJs play a great ever-changing selection of alternative music. As one review of the bar states: '8MM is the perfect place to make out with a rockstar.'

Schönhauser Allee 177b, 10119 Prenzlauer Berg, 8mmbar.de

Schwarz Sauer

A cosy old school Berlin bar with a huge terrace, Schwarz Sauer is the platonic ideal of a Berlin summer spot with a good selection of tap beer, affordable wine, and decent whiskey. Come here for a fun night out with a group of friends to discuss important life issues deep into the night.

Kastanienallee 13, 10435 Prenzlauer Berg

Haliflor

Another comforting bar in the heart of Berlin. Haliflor's façade is reminiscent of Hopper's *Nighthawks* and truly feels like a place outside of time and space. The drinks are reasonably priced, and the atmosphere is lively without being overbearing. Perfect if you are looking for a calmer night out.

Schwedter Strasse 26, 10119 Prenzlauer Berg, haliflor.com

Supamolly

An iconic and long-standing Berlin punk bar, at Supamolly the drinks are cheap, the music is loud, and the bar keepers are not afraid to speak their mind. A stereotypical Berlin punk bar as good as they come.

Jessnerstrasse 41, 10247 Friedrichshain, supamolly.de

Primitiv Bar

This unique and inviting bar is filled with sofas, offering plenty of cosy seats for you and your friends. The music selection consists primarily of 60s and 70s garage rock oddities. Primitiv Bar is also the occasional host of Thirsty Thursdays. This semi-comedic reading of fictitious erotica is great for a drink and a good laugh.

Simon-Dach-Strasse 28, 10245 Friedrichshain, insta @primitiv_bar

Urban Spree

A great music venue for underground gigs, Urban Spree usually offers affordable concerts with bands from all over the world. In summer, they open their lively beer garden in addition to their usual indoor bar area. As it's also a music venue, drinks aren't as cheap as they are in other bars but prices are still reasonable. Come here if you want to catch a great new musical act.

Revaler Strasse 99, 10245 Friedrichshain, urbanspree.com

Franken Bar

Possibly the best place to get an affordable pint of Guinness in Berlin, Franken offers a great selection of beers on tap as well as cocktails, and plays some of the finest rock and punk classics. The interior is great for small groups with plenty of large sofas and tables. Their toilets are quite peculiar, as they are incredibly spacious and maze-like, almost reminiscent of the halls of a Victorian sanatorium.

Oranienstrasse 19a, 10999 Kreuzberg, franken-bar.de

Cafe Kotti

Located in the bustling heart of Kreuzberg, Cafe Kotti is a true melting pot of Berlin's numerous scenes. The clientele are primarily students, but it is also frequented by cab drivers and neighbours. Since the cafe is located on the first floor of its building, the terrace offers a great view of the bustling Kottbusser Tor. A great and foremost cheap establishment, Cafe Kotti is the perfect place to listen to a good story from a stranger or have a laugh with your friends.

Adalbertstrasse 96b, 10999 Kreuzberg

Taqueria Florian

Contrary to what the name might suggest, no tacos can be found at Taqueria Florian. But what they do serve, is even better: affordable wines and beers. Located right opposite the world famous SO36 music club, Taqueria Florian is a cosy neighbourhood smokers bar. In summer, their large terrace is a great place to enjoy a nice glass of *Rose* and immersive yourself in the ever-busy atmosphere of Berlin's streets.

Oranienstrasse 17, 10999 Kreuzberg

Ankerklause

Beloved by all who are fortunate enough to live near, Ankerklause is another Berlin classic. Come here for a tasty affordable

portion of fish & chips while you gaze at the swans swimming the Spree. If you wish to do as the locals do, order yourself a *Berliner Weisse* (opt for green over red for the classic experience) and be amazed by this Berlin peculiarity.

Kottbusser Damm 104, 10967 Kreuzberg / Neukölln, ankerklause.de

Loophole

An institution of the Berlin underground scene, Loophole boasts an impressive back catalogue of underground acts and DJs. The small, grungy interior is split into two by a heavy curtain separating the dancefloor and stage from the main seating area. Usually jam-packed and the perfect place to catch local as well as international bands and dance the night away.

Boddinstrasse 60, 12053 Neukölln, loophole.berlin

Schankwirtschaft Laidak

A great cafe and bar, Laidak is great for smokers and non-smokers alike, as the bar is split up into two distinct areas. In the smoky backroom, you are greeted by an inviting warm light and encouraged to peruse the shelves stocked to the brim with card and board games. A great location for a game of chess and a glass of wine at a reasonable price. Considering its price, their coffee is also notably good.

Boddinstrasse 42/43, 12053 Neukölln, laidak.net

Heiners Bar

Perhaps Berlin's most beautiful bar, the ornate, dark wooden counter stands as the centrepiece of the large maze-like interior. Heiners has a good selection of beers on tap and wines, and offers plenty of seating. Come here for the beautiful interior and stay for the cold drinks and intoxicating atmosphere.

Weserstrasse 58, 12045 Neukölln

Tennis Bar

A quirky little establishment, Tennis Bar hosts a series of events, ranging from karaoke and country nights to album release parties, and fundraisers. They also have the occasional food pop-up event where you can find a delicious meal at a great price. A true all-rounder with something in store for everyone.

Reuterstrasse 95, 12053 Neukölln,
insta @tennisbarberlin

CLUBS

Berlin is famous for its clubbing scene. In 2024, Berlin techno was even awarded UNESCO World Heritage status. There are numerous clubs as well as unregulated parties and events that change venues. Tip: when walking around Berlin, look on the traffic light poles for stickers promoting current events.

Things to bring to a techno party: sunglasses, a handheld fan, gum, and some water. And not just for yourself; there will be lots of others asking you for any of them. Making new friends couldn't be easier! Berlin offers many options, such as RSO, Club OST, Renate, Kater Blau, Turbulence TXL, and Kitkat, but we'll describe five of the most famous techno clubs.

Tresor

The oldest club in Berlin, Tresor was one of the main players in creating the techno scene. They started out in the vaults of an abandoned warehouse, later moving its location to a power station in Mitte.

Köpenicker Strasse 70, 10179 Mitte,
tresorberlin.com

Berghain

This club is known for its strict dress code and selective entry policy. Berghain is arguably one of the most popular clubs worldwide and also one of the most mysterious. Only those who get in will discover what happens inside: taking pictures or making videos is strictly against the rules. When we think of Berghain outfits, we think of all black leather. Above all, Berghain is a gay club meant to foster self-expression, and dressing authentically may offer the best chance to experience it firsthand.

Am Wriezener Bahhof, 10243 Friedrichshain, berghain.berlin

Sisyphos

Sisyphos, located in Friedrichs-hain, offers a more colourful take on techno parties, ditching the unofficial all black dress code. It features multiple stages hosting different types of techno and house, along with an outside area that includes a pond and a small beach. Some nights are 21+.

Haupstrasse 15, 10317 Friedrichshain, sisyphos-berlin.net

Cassiopeia

Hip-Hop, 80s, 90s or even live concerts, Cassiopeia schedules a broad range of music. Weather permitting, you can enjoy their biergarten while taking your pick from the different foods on offer. The large club, with its three different floors, is located at R.A.W, a former 'National Railway Repair Works' (see page 63).

Revaler Straße 99, 10245 Friedrichshain, cassiopeia-berlin.de

Spindler und Klatt

This is an intimate venue, with a capacity of just 200 partygoers, right next to the Spree. You can grab a bite to eat before partying on the rooftop terrace. Spindler und Klatt offer various nights, from Hip-Hop and RnB throw-backs to a K-Pop night, there is something for everyone. Check the club agenda on their website and Instagram; make sure you carefully check ticket prices and age requirements.

Köpenicker Straße 16, 10997 Kreuzberg, spindlerklatt.com

Engtanz

Engtanz is a party that
happens roughly once a month
in various German cities,
including Berlin. With classic
English language 'house party'
songs that everyone will know.
They announce dates and
venues on their Instagram and
mailing list.

insta @iloveengtanz

Toy Tonics

Techno can be perceived as a
'darker' genre. For those who
prefer upbeat disco and house
music, Toy Tonics is the way
to go. Their crew tours around
Europe, but they often return
to Berlin. The dates can be
found on their Instagram and
in the newsletter. To get in
the mood, they have weekly
updated playlists on Spotify
@Toy Tonics.

insta @toytonics

SHOPPING

HOW TO DRESS LIKE A LOCAL

Blend in with the locals and dress like a typical Berliner by incorporating a few of these items into your outfit. The first rule applies to everyone, androgynous styles rule.

A woollen beanie is an accessory you will see the locals wearing 365 days a year. Yes, even in hot summers you'll see people wearing beanies, although less often than in winter, of course. And wear glasses, even if you don't need them.

There is not really such a thing as an it-bag in Berlin. Go for a tote, preferably with a rebellious quote or one from a vegan farmers market. Our favourite: the totes from the magazine and bookstore do you read me?!

Choose your jeans carefully, they should be dark, and they might be a little on the short side. Go for a sustainable brand or buy them second-hand.

Don't worry too much about your shoes. No high heels, sometimes the pavements are a bit uneven. Dr. Martens or similar will do the trick. And yes, they do pair very well with shorts and skirts. In summer, you could switch to Birkenstocks, preferably the Arizona. And don't be afraid to wear them with socks if it's chilly. Birkenstock clogs also work for autumn or spring.

To truly blend in, always have a bottle of beer or Club-Mate in your hand when walking around town. Leave the empty bottle at any litter bin (see page 92).

13

FLEA MARKETS, VINTAGE & SECOND-HAND

FLEA MARKETS

On Sundays, the favourite pastime of many Berliners is to browse flea markets. We'll list the classics, although there are a lot more options.

Trödelmarkt Arkonaplatz

Arkonaplatz, 10435 Mitte

A small, lively, and very cosy flea market. You can buy clothes, accessories, home goods, antiques, vintage, and DDR goodies. Like at most flea markets in Berlin, stalls are run by a mix of professional and private sellers. Combine a stroll along this market with a visit to nearby Mauerpark. Sundays from 10am to 5pm, 10am to 4pm in winter.

Mauerpark

Bernauer Strasse 63-64 (entrance), 13355 Mitte, flohmarktimmauerpark.de

The Sunday flea market in Mauerpark really is something special. There are endless rows of stalls, attracting a large crowd. It has a great vibe, and is excellent for shopping for cheap clothes, vinyl, and all kinds of accessories. The many food stalls alone are worth a visit. Most Sundays, from 10am to 6pm.

Boxhagener Platz

Boxhagener Platz 1, 10245 Friedrichshain

Similar to Arkonaplatz, this is a small but very friendly flea market. It is great for treasure hunting and offers especially good hunting grounds for books and vinyl. Sundays 10am to 6pm.

Nowkoelln Flowmarkt

Maybachufer 32-33, 12047 Neukölln, nowkoelln.de

A lot of second-hand, art, vinyl, handmade goodies, and much, much more. There are 130 stalls, mostly run by private sellers. March to October every other Sunday from 10am to. Check the website for details. Twice a week you'll find a *Stoffmarkt*, where you can buy fabrics as well as vinyl and DDR memorabilia.

Schoeneboerg Flowmarkt

Crellemarktplatz, 10827 Schöneberg, schoeneboerg.de

Sister of the Nowkoelln Flowmarkt, near S-Bahn station Yorckstrasse, it offers similar goods: second-hand, handmade treasures, and lots of art and vinyl. March to October every other Sunday from 10 – alternates weeks with Nowkoelln. Check the website for details.

Rathaus Schöneberg

John-F.-Kenndyplatz 1, 10825 Schöneberg

At first glance, this may seem like an enormous square filled with the contents of a gazillion rubbish bins. But if you're a seasoned second-hand hunter, you won't leave empty handed. Every Saturday and Sunday 8am to 4pm.

VINTAGE & SECOND-HAND

There are many (MANY!) vintage shops in Berlin. Most shops in Mitte and Prenzlauer Berg sell somewhat more expensive finds. Good examples are Garments (Linienstrasse) and Das Neue Schwarz (Mulackstrasse). Neukölln is the best area for second-hand shops.

Humana Secondhand

humana.com

With shops scattered all over the city, Humana is a great chain for thrifting second-hand clothes and accessories at low prices. All open Mondays to Saturdays 10am to 8pm. Short on time? Head directly to the branch at Alexanderstrasse (Mitte) or Frankfurter Tor (Friedrichshain), those are the biggest. If you're a 'lazy' second-hand shopper, opt for the stores with curated items.

Vintage Revivals

Schönhauser Allee 127, 10437 Mitte / Münzstrasse 5, 10178 Mitte, vintagerevivals.de

One of our favourites in town, with two shops close to each other in Mitte. Not truly old vintage-vintage but second-hand from around the 70s, 80s, and onward. This is preloved fashion at its best.

Picknweight

Alte Schönhauserstrasse 30, 10178 Mitte / Münzstrasse 19, 10178 Mitte, picknweight.de

Familiar with the kilo shop concept? This is basically the same: you weigh the items at checkout. But not every item has the same price, so keep an eye on the tags. Students receive a 10% discount.

Who Killed Bambi?

An der Spandauer Brücke 10, 10178 Mitte

In this shop, you'll find a nice mixture of new and second-hand clothes and accessories, many of them very colourful.

Paul's Boutique

Oderbergerstrasse 47, 10435 Prenzlauer Berg, paulsboutiqueberlin.de

Hundreds of trainers in the shop window and even more inside, that's what Paul's is famous for. Take your time and you will find your next pair of Adidas, Nike, or New Balance kicks. Be prepared to dig: the models are stacked up high. Paul's Boutique also has a shop in Mitte.

Goo

Oderbergerstrasse 45, 10435 Prenzlauer Berg, paulsboutiqueberlin.de

Next to Paul's Boutique, and from the same owner, you'll find Goo. This shop specialises in second-hand designer brands. Definitely not the cheapest, but an awesome place to go if you've saved up to treat yourself to something special.

V Vintage Fashion

Kopernikusstrasse 18, 10245 Friedrichshain, insta @v_vintagefashionberlin

Big knitted jumpers in old-school patterns, woollen hats, sweaters, T-shirts, shoes. Looking for that 80s vibe? You'll find it here. We love the outfits on their Instagram feed.

Koku Secondhand Store

Schillerpromenade 1, 12049 Neukölln, insta @ kokusecondhand

Did we mention Dr. Martens? And how Berliners are inseparable from a good pair? Head to Koku to buy them second-hand. An incredible number of boots is waiting for their next owner. Could it be you?

Let Them Eat Cake

Weserstrasse 164, 12045 Neukölln, insta @ ltec_berlin

Named after the famous phrase Marie-Antoinette allegedly uttered in the 18th century (spoiler alert: this was probably untrue). Both an art space and a vintage store, this is a great combination, with a nice collection of clothes too.

Loppis

Weserstrasse 167, 12045 Neukölln, insta @ loppisvintageberlin

Since the Swedish name for flea market is *loppis*, the collection at Loppis is distinctly Scandinavian. No 80s disco prints here, but calm and minimalist Nordic style clothing.

Not too sweet

Bürknerstrasse 6, 12047 Neukölln, nottoosweetvintage.com

Do you feel like buying a Y2K or Dolce & Gabbana item? Look no further. Besides vintage, they also sell some upcycled or 'reworked' items at Not too sweet. A small but usually interesting collection.

Veist

Selchower Strasse 32, 12049 Neuköllnn, veistberlin.com

According to Veist, every piece of clothing has a story to tell. No anonymous clothes in here, but each piece has a little story attached to them. They also sell some nicely upcycled pieces.

Yummy Vintage

Bürknerstrasse 12, 12047 Neukölln, insta @ yummyvintageofficial

A beautiful vintage shop with high-quality items and a lovely staff. Come here if you are looking for something to make your outfit shine.

STREETWEAR

Civilist

Brunnenstrasse 13, 10119 Mitte, civilistberlin.com

There are many skate shops in Berlin, most of which can be found in Kreuzberg. Civilist, in Mitte, stocks local brand Backbone of Berlin.

Souvenir official

Torstrasse 76, 10119 Mitte, souvenirofficial.com

A politically focused, young Berlin brand. Keep an eye out for the Eunify sweaters and T-shirts featuring the European flag with a missing little star as a nod to Brexit.

Superconscious

Weinbergsweg 22 and Torstrasse 72, 10119 Mitte, superconscious.de

A very cool shop, or shops in fact, with brands that are 'ahead of their time'. They stock underground brands from all over the world.

↓ SUPREME

Supreme

Torstrasse 74, 10119 Berlin, supreme.com

Supreme is not always open, and sometimes there's even a queue to get in, but this expensive skate brand is still very popular. It is also good to just browse for inspiration.

Comme des Garçons

Linienstrasse 115, 10115 Mitte, comme-des-garcons.de

Dreaming of a pair of Converse with the funny love heart? Then head for the only CDG store in Germany. They sell their own lines as well as streetwear by other brands.

SNS

Schönhauser Allee 6-7, 10119 Mitte, sneakersnstuff.com

A good selection of popular streetwear brands with a focus on trainers, with some nice collaborations thrown in. And, while you're there; PastaBar across the street serves great pasta!

Voo Store

Oranienstrasse 24, 10999 Kreuzberg, vooberlin.com

Slightly hidden from the street, in a so-called *Hinterhof* (backyard), you find this well-known address for designer clothing. They have a beautiful collection, and a café too.

Zebraclub

Zossenerstrasse 37, 10961 Kreuzberg, zebraclub.store

Zebraclub has three locations (one of which is only open on Saturdays), that are all equally good for trainers, jeans, and streetwear. The address given is 'the busy one', according to the owners.

R.T.C.O.

Sanderstrasse 6, 12047 Neukölln, r-t-co-com.

The name is short for Rollo T-shirt COmpany, stemming back to a time when they just sold handprinted T-shirts. Now, they sell T-shirts, cool sunglasses, and even their own skate deck.

DEPARTMENT STORES

Mall of Berlin

*Leipziger Strasse 12, 10117
Mitte, mallofberlin.de*

This is a mall like they have in the U.S.A. Shiny floors, a lot of glass and many, many shops spread out on four levels. Ideal for a cold or rainy day.

Scheunenviertel

Scheunenviertel, Mitte

If you want to browse some special shops, just mark these streets in Mitte on your map: Alte Schönhauser Strasse, Rosenthaler Strasse, Weinmeisterstrasse, and Münzstrasse. In the same part of Mitte, Torstrasse and Weinbergsweg also have some nice shops.

**Kurfürstendamm &
Tauentzienstrasse**

*Kurfürstendamm /
Tauentzienstrasse,
Charlottenburg*

Looking for the bigger, well-known brands? Go to Kurfurstendamm, also known as Ku'damm. It's a super busy shopping street with the likes of Chanel, Cartier, and Valentino (great for window shopping) but also some more affordable brands. Shops like Uniqlo, Adidas, and Nike can also be found in this area.

Bikini Berlin

*Budapesterstrasse 38,
10787 Charlottenburg,
bikiniberlin.de*

Pop-up store galore! Not the cheapest, but you'll find some very nice shops selling clothes from Berlin based designers. It is close to the Zoo and its abundance of restaurants makes it a nice visit.

KaDeWe

Tauentzienstrasse 21-24, 10789 Charlottenburg, kadewe.de

The interior of KaDeWe, short for Kaufhaus des Westens, is beautiful – check out the ceilings and the wooden escalators. The first five floors are reserved for cosmetics, men's and women's clothing, a 'kids world' and home decor. The sixth and seventh floor are devoted to food and delicacies. (Please note: At the time of writing, it is unclear whether the bankruptcy of KaDeWe will result in the shop being closed permanently or they will reopen.)

Manufactum

Hardenbergerstrasse 4-5, 10623 Charlottenburg, manufactum.de

Expensive, but beautiful. Manufactum sells old fashioned German (and other European) products like Bavarian woollen coats, children's games, and lovely towels to upgrade your bathroom. If you're interested in cooking, do check the shelves with beautiful pots and pans. Treat yourself to something small, like a new sketchbook, as a nice souvenir.

Muji

Kurfürstendamm 236, 10719 Charlottenburg / Hackescher Markt 1, 10178 Mitte, germany.muji.eu

This Japanese store sells gorgeous, minimalist basics. They have a large selection for travellers, including packing cubes, but to us, their stationery is the main attraction. The shelves with coloured pens, pencils, notebooks, and small organizers for school or university are the best. They also sell a selection of unisex clothing.

BOOKSHOPS

Buchbox

buchboxberlin.de

A small chain of bookshops, located in Prenzlauer Berg as well as Kreuzberg. The one at Kastanienallee 88 is called LoveStory Berlin and has a selection of English books and small gifts. The shop at Kastanienallee 97 is also wonderful for books lovers, while the other shops are more focused on German literature and children's books.

do you read me?!

Auguststrasse 28, 10117 Mitte, doyoureadme.de

Graphic designer Mark Kiessling opened this fantastic little bookshop. They have a great selection of books on art, architecture, photography, graphic design, and much more, as well as lots of international magazines. Don't leave without the iconic tote, and don't forget to thank us later.

Dussman

Friedrichstrasse 90, 10117 Mitte, kulturkaufhaus.de

Das Kulturkaufhaus, or: the cultural superstore of Berlin. In the back of the ground floor, you'll find the entrance to the English bookshop. Its selection is almost overwhelming. Downstairs offers literature and YA, while upstairs you can browse all other genres. Dussmann has a second location at the Sony Center at Potsdamer Platz, where they sell books as well as merchandise for film enthusiasts.

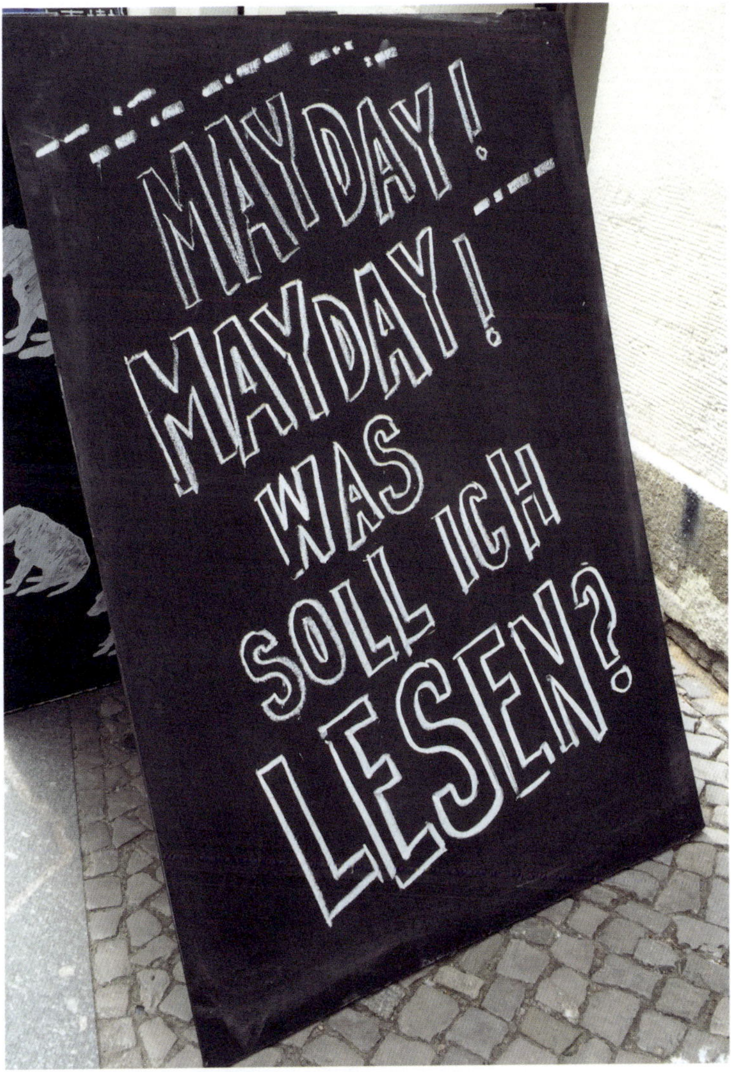
MAYDAY!
MAYDAY!
WAS
SOLL ICH
LESEN?

Hundt Hammer Stein

Alte Schönhauser Strasse 23/24, 10119 Mitte, hundthammerstein.de

A pleasant little bookshop hidden in a basement. They stock German literature as well as English fiction and non-fiction. Take in the recommendations – or non-recommendations – on the books, which can be hilarious. If you are just in the market for a postcard, this is your spot too.

Ocelot, not just another bookstore

Brunnenstrasse 181, 10119 Mitte, insta @ocelotberlin

The atmosphere is what makes this shop so pleasurable. Their book selection is not even that large, but it is very well curated. They sell very nice paper goodies and a great selection of books about Berlin. Coffee and drinks can be ordered at the bar and enjoyed at the large communal table.

Shakespeare and Sons

Warschauer Strasse 74, 10243 Friedrichshain, shakespeareandsons.com

Not only an independent bookstore, but a very nice bagel shop too. An ideal combination for hours of book shopping. The collection is both second-hand and new, with a focus on fiction, non-fiction, and YA. Open daily from 8am to 7pm.

Berlin Book Nook

Pflügerstrasse 63, 12047 Neukölln, theberlinbooknook.blogspot.com

This book nook stocks over 6,000 titles for next to nothing. Don't visit this second-hand bookshop when you're in a hurry, as you will want to check them all out.

Kohlhaas & Co.

Fasanenstrasse 23,
10719 Charlottenburg,
kohlhaasbuch.de

Sometimes location is everything. This bookshop is based in Literaturhaus Berlin, a beautiful house with an even more beautiful garden. Read all about its history on the website and go there for the great book selection.

Marga Schoeller
Bücherstube

Knesebeckstrasse 33,
10623 Charlottenburg,
margaschoeller.de

A bookshop with a great selection of English books, as well as some English literary magazines like *SAND*, the Berlin made magazine for literature and art. Tell them what you're looking for, and they will find it for you.

Bücherbogen am
Savignyplatz

Stadtbahnbogen 593,
10623 Charlottenburg,
buecherbogen.com

A beautiful bookshop beneath S-Bahnstation Savignyplatz. Don't just browse the books, explore the bookshop itself, as it is an interesting building. There is a lot of literature to be found, as well as a great selection of art books.

Saint George's

Wörther Strasse 27,
10405 Prenzlauer Berg,
saintgeorgesbookshop.com

Named after the Patron Saint of England, this English bookshop stocks a huge array of second-hand books. They have new stock coming in from England regularly. From classics to romcoms and poetry: you can find just about anything here.

She Said

Kottbusser Damm 79,
10967 Kreuzberg,
shesaid.de

A bookshop that only sells books written by female or queer authors, featuring diverse and unique voices that may get overshadowed in bigger shops. You can even grab a coffee and read your new purchase while you're there, as there's also a nice cafe.

ART SUPPLIES

R.S.V.P. in Mitte

*Mulackstrasse 26, 10119
Mitte, rsvp-berlin.de*

Are you into journaling, a lover of beautiful paper goodies, or just in need of a new calendar? Do you want to send your secret love a beautiful postcard? R.S.V.P. is your place to go. It is also a must-visit for masking tape collectors. A Kaweco fountain pen makes for a great gift to yourself.

Frau Tulpe Stoffe

*Veteranenstrasse 19, 10119
Mitte, frautulpe.de*

Looking for some fabric to make your own tote? Frau Tulpe stocks some beautiful patterns. She also sells starter kits, for those who are just taking their first steps into creating something. Please note, the shop is only open Thursdays to Saturdays.

Modulor

*Prinzenstrasse 85, 10969
Kreuzberg, modulor.de*

One of the biggest, brightest, and most colourful shops around. Two floors of paints, paper, pencils, beautiful stationery, and all kinds of other art supplies. Modulor is based in the Aufbau Haus at Moritzplatz, the U-bahn stops right underneath. The Aufbau Haus also houses a great bookshop and a café named Rock-Paper, for tasty cakes and coffee.

CYM
Kunstmalerbedarf
---
*Dieffenbachstrasse 16
and Planufer 96, 10967
Kreuzberg,
cym-kunstmalerbedarf.de*

Fadeninsel
---
*Oranienstrasse 23, 10999
Kreuzberg, fadeninsel.de*

Better Run
---
*Hasselwerderstrasse 37,
12439 Neukölln,
betterrun.shop*

Idee.
---
*Joachimsthaler Strasse
41, 10623 Charlottenburg,
idee-shop.com*

Two shops with the same name, both very good for art supplies. Even if it is just the best blue paint, some new brushes, or a few pencils you're after. The staff is super friendly and very helpful.

Knitting or crocheting on your mind? Head for Fadeninsel. They have sold a lot of wool ever since they opened in 2002, mostly the natural kind. In case you want to start right away, they sell patterns and needles too.

Feeling inspired by Berlin's street art? At some places you can just spray away (see *paintyourfirstgraffiti.com*) but seek advice before you find yourself in the hands of the police. Better Run is dedicated to spray cans and markers; they sell hundreds. The store is a little out of the way but can be reached by S-Bahn Schöneweide.

Another all-in-one shop for the creative crowd. They sell everything for those who want to paint or work with fabric, those who just want to write in their journal, and those in need of new stickers too. Two additional locations in Berlin.

AFFORDABLE ART AND HOME DECO

Schee

Rosenthaler Strasse 15,
10119 Mitte, schee.shop

No matter how small your room, there is always an empty spot. The walls of Schee are covered in prints that are available in various sizes. They also have a selection of smaller items like pens, coffee cups, funny gifts, and stationery.

Superbazaro

Mulackstrasse 1,
10119 Mitte,
insta @superbazaromitte

Just around the corner of restaurant Mädchenitaliener (nice!) you'll find this small shop, packed with lots and lots of gifts, interior decoration, accessories, books, delicacies, and chocolate (Italian, of course). We especially like the postcards and the garlands, as every day should be a party.

VEB Orange

Oderbergerstrasse 29,
10435 Prenzlauer Berg,
insta @veb_orange

If you're into DDR-memorabilia, you must head to this small shop close to Mauerpark. It can be a bit overwhelming at first: it is filled from floor to ceiling with, well, anything. From lamps to chairs, but also magazines, small Fernsehtürme and much more. Take your time, it's a fun shop to browse.

Supalife Kiosk

*Raumerstrasse 40, 10437
Prenzlauer Berg,
supalife.de*

This small shop lives and breathes creativity, speaking to your inner artist. Supalife is the best address in Berlin for (screen) prints, big and small. The smaller ones are usually quite affordable. They also stock a good selection of postcards. Everything in the shop is made by Berlin-based creatives.

Cuongs Creative Market

*Wrangelstrasse 76,
10997 Kreuzberg,
cuongscreativemarket.com*

Another spot for prints, this time in Kreuzberg. Various illustrators, designers, and artists, all based in Berlin, sell their prints in this shop, set up by Cuong Bui Manh. For smaller budgets, the prints also come postcard sized.

Hallesches Haus

*Tempelhofer Ufer 1, 10961
Kreuzberg,
hallescheshaus.com*

Location is key, and Hallesches Haus has a beautiful setting. They sell a wide range of items, like candles, books, stationery, homeware, and some clothing. What's not to like? Even if you don't find anything to your liking, it is still highly recommended for breakfast or lunch.

Wohnzimmer 36

*Paul-Linck-Ufer 44,
10999 Kreuzberg,
wohnzimmer36.de
hallescheshaus.com*

A colourful store with gifts and gadgets like candles, cushions, vases, and key chains. They also sell bags and backpacks at Wohnzimmer 36, and they have a nice selection of postcards and paper goodies.

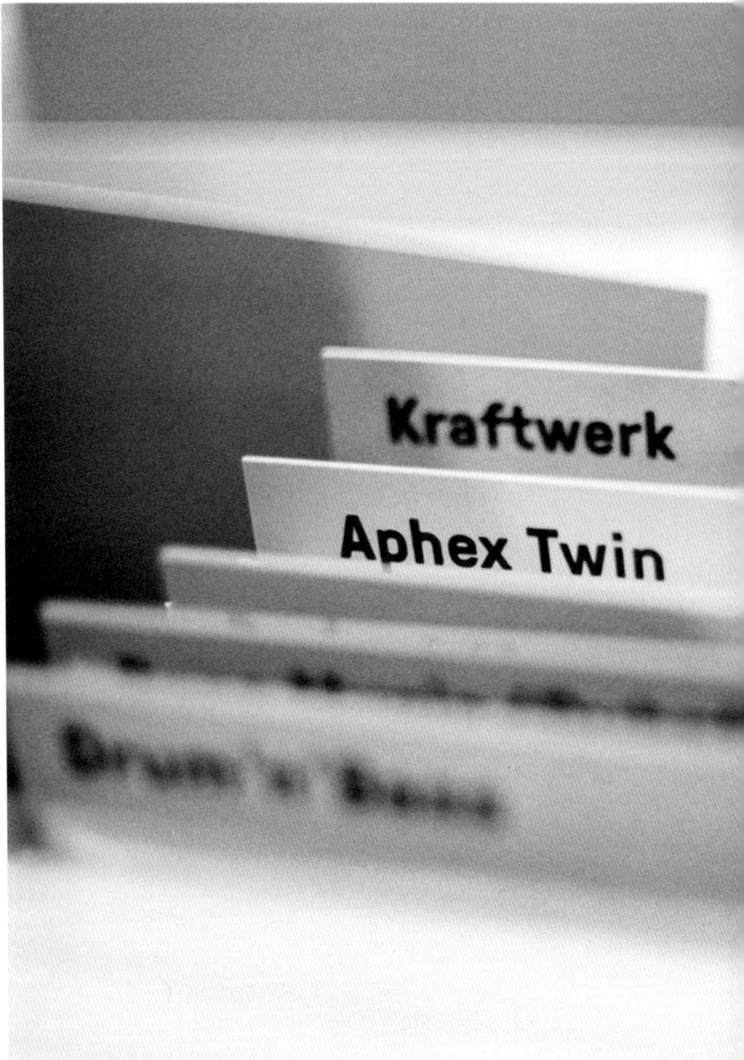
Kraftwerk
Aphex Twin

RECORD SHOPS

The Record Store

Invalidenstrasse 148,
10115 Mitte

They have been selling new and second-hand vinyl at this place for over twenty years. The friendly staff and the selection of music from all eras makes this one of the best places in town to find rare records.

Melting Point Record Store

Kastanienallee 55, 10119 Prenzlauer Berg, insta @ melt.ingpointrecordstore

A good selection and good prices, all you really need from a record shop. And here you have it. They stock both new and second-hand vinyl, including lots of disco and house.

Hard Wax

Köpenicker Strasse 70, 10179 Kreuzberg

This record shop is a mecca for techno lovers, next-door to the infamous techno club Tresor. It is also the right place for reggae, dub, and dubstep. Added bonus: they also sell vinyl from Berliner record labels.

CD shop ZeeDee

Brüsseler Strasse 4, 13353 Wedding (north from Mitte), zeedee-shop.com

Second-hand CDs are much cheaper than used vinyl, so it might be a good idea to buy a CD-player and start your collection here. Over 60,000 used CDs are for sale, so make sure you have plenty of time to browse the entire shop. It is a little bit out of the city centre: take the U-Bahn to Seestrasse.

SHOPS WE LOVE

Herr Nilsson

herrnilsson.com

Forget gummy bears (okay, maybe not). If you crave sweets, head to Herr Nilsson — indeed named after Pippi Longstocking's pet monkey — for rows and rows of sweet and sour sweets, chocolates, licorice, and more. They also stock vegetarian and vegan options. Fill a glass jar or paper bag to take home, but we doubt if the contents will make it that far. Based on three locations in Berlin: two in Prenzlauer Berg, and one in Friedrichshain.

↓ TUKADU

↓ S.WERT

S.Wert

Brunnenstrasse 191, 10119 Mitte, s-wert.de

This shop is filled with Berlin's icons. With or without the Fernsehturm, posters, postcards, cushions, and tea towels are everywhere. They sell a card game with all of Berlin's bars, pens, temporary tattoos, buttons ... you name it. Skip the typical tourist shops and head straight to this one.

Tukadu

Rosenthalerstrasse 46/47, 10178 Mitte, tukadu.com

A cheerful shop for colourful, one-of-a-kind jewellery, with collections aptly named Kreuzberger Chic and Berlin Beat. Bling and glass beads are combined with tiny plastic animals. Not the cheapest pieces, but you can buy most beads and figurines by the piece and create your own earrings and necklaces. They also offer a complete DIY-set.

Brettspielgeschäft

Eberswalderstrasse 27, 10437 Prenzlauer Berg, shop.brettspielgeschaeft. berlin

Get offline and play a board game. Treat yourself to something beyond the good old chess board, though they sell those at Brettspielgeschäft too. This shop sells over 3,000 games, 1,000 of those in English, from history games to war games, from family games to spy games. Go and see it for yourself.

Zauberkönig

Herrfurthstrasse 6a, 12049 Neukölln, zauberkoenig-berlin.de

Unleash your inner Fred and George: this shop is reminiscent of Weasley's Wizard Wheezes in Diagon Alley. They sell anything you might need for Halloween or to just make you feel like a child again. It is also a great place to find souvenirs younger family members.

GREEN BERLIN

DO YOU READ ME?!

PARKS AND SWIMMING

Berliner Bäder

berlinerbaeder.de

In summer, Berliners tend to swim in nearby lakes. But during the cold winter months, a beautiful indoor pool is a much better plan. Stadtbad Mitte, dating back to 1930, is a classic. Another beauty is Stadtbad Neukölln. But the very best you'll find in Hotel Stadtbad Oderberger in Prenzlauer Berg. Swimming might not be the first thing on your mind for your visit, but now you'll know where to go.

Tiergarten Park

Strasse des 17. Juni, 10785 Tiergarten / Mitte

Green lungs are important for any city. London has Hyde Park, New York has Central Park, and Berlin has Tiergarten Park. After World War II, Tiergarten Park was completely bare. All the trees were cut as their wood was needed for heating. It is hard to imagine, as Tiergarten is now the largest and greenest park of Berlin.

Monbijou Park

Oranienburgerstrasse, 10178 Mitte

One of the smaller parks of the city, but such a charmer. Next to the Museumsinsel and the river Spree, this is the perfect place for a picnic in the grass. In summer, the park is brimming with cultural activities, including late night dancing. Even if you're not into salsa, it is fun to watch everyone having a good time. Several Spätis in the streets fringing the park sell drinks, and if you're lucky the kiosk is open too.

Mauerpark

Bernauer Strasse /
Eberswalderstrasse,
10437 Prenzlauer Berg,
mauerpark.info

Mauerpark is probably Berlin's most famous, as it is in a part of town that used to be one of the death strips of the Berlin Wall. Known for its large graffiti wall, its Sunday Flohmarkt and karaoke, it is also a lovely green, open space to spend an afternoon. The park is quite big: it's best to take the U2 to Eberswalderstrasse or the M10 (tram) to Wolliner Strasse.

Freiluftkino

freiluftkino-berlin.de

At three locations in Berlin (Friedrichshain, Kreuzberg, and Rehberge) you can watch films in the open air, the so-called *Freiluftkino*. Films are shown throughout the summer. It is a lovely experience, but don't forget to bring a blanket and mosquito repellent. Check the programme carefully, as most films are in German. It is advisable to book ahead, as these screenings are massively popular.

Volkspark Friedrichshain

Am Friedrichshain 1,
10407 Friedrichshain

You'll find a lot of families strolling through this park, as there are many playgrounds and sports facilities. Built in 1840, it was the first park for the people of Berlin. You can check out the Märchenbrunnen (Fairytale Fountain) or climb one of the two hills that are built on rubble from World War II. The park also has a pleasant biergarten, Schoenbrunn, with a little kiosk for takeaway drinks and snacks.

Park am Gleisdreieck

Möckernstrasse 26,
10963 Kreuzberg,
parkamgleisdreieck.de

This park is dedicated to activities like beach volleyball, skating, football, and basketball. But it's lovely if you're just planning to have a little picnic or a stroll as well. Next to this park, you'll find the Dora-Duncker-Park, where former wasteland is turned into an urban green spot. If you want to delve deeper, follow the Storywalk Gleisdreieck. Its 27 stops teach you more about urban nature.

Tempelhofer Feld

Oderstrasse/
Herrfurthstrasse,
12049 Neukölln,
tempelhoferfeld.de

It's clear, we can't get enough of Tempelhofer Feld. Apart from a very good photo spot (see page 97), it is also a place to relax and have a picnic. Ideal for lazy afternoons on the grass, strolling over its former runway. Bring your bike or skateboard, explore the area, but don't expect trees. The park is open until sunset, or a little before. Summer is an excellent time to visit as the park remains open until 11pm (and it opens at 6am, if you're that much of an early bird).

Treptower Park

Am Treptower Park 20,
12435 Treptow-Köpen

This park along the Spree has so much to see, it is more of a cultural spot than a place for relaxation. There is a huge Soviet War Memorial, a symbol for the contribution of Russia in the defeat of the Nazis. The park is also home to the Archenhold Observatory, the oldest and biggest planetarium of Germany. If you want to explore the water, you can hire a boat from Kanuliebe. You can find this park outside the city centre, south of Kreuzberg/Friedrichshain.

VEGETARIAN AND VEGAN BERLIN

Berlin is said to be the vegan capital of Europe. And it's true: it's a plant-based paradise. If you check *happycow.net*, over 1,600 options for vegetarians and vegans pop up. Most restaurants offer vegetarian and vegan options, but these focus solely on the plant-based variety. Some places stand out, others are worth a visit for other reasons too. Some sweet, some savoury, some for breakfast, some for lunch and dinner, but always good. There are countless ice cream parlours that sell vegan ice creams as well.

Brammibal's Donuts

Living as a vegan equals life without cake? No way! At Brammibal's Donuts you can have vegan donuts. When you take a closer look at them, they are more like little cakes. You can choose lemon cheesecake, raspberry pistachio, or the 'common' cinnamon sugar donut.

brammibalsdonuts.com

Haferkater

If you need a quick breakfast, head to one of the four locations of Haferkater. Porridge it is! With toppings like fruit, cookies, and chocolate. The one on Friedrichtstrasse is the most centrally located.

haferkater.com

Organic supermarkets

There are plenty of organic supermarkets in Berlin, such as Bio Company, Denns, Alnatura, and LPG. Some sell meat, most of them lots of vegetables. And: salads,quiches and the like, ideal for a picnic in the park. No need to give you the address, as these chains can be found all over the city.

Veg'd

Longing for a good burger? The No-Beef-Patty is the specialty of Veg'd. They serve juicy burgers, loaded fries, onion rings, and nuggets. It looks a bit like that fast-food chain with the golden arches, but this is ten times better. Check out their seasonal specials or lunch deals, when they offer a burger with fries for less than 11 euros. At four locations in Berlin (Kreuzberg, Friedrichshain and Prenzlauer Berg).

vegd.eu

The Butterfly Lovers

You won't find any Peking Duck in here, as this modern and bright Chinese restaurant is completely vegan. It is known for its tasty salads, but the eggplant dishes also come recommended.

Veteranenstrasse 10, 10119 Mitte, insta @ the.butterflylovers

FREA Bakery

Zero waste, local, and plant-based: it won't get more environmentally friendly than FREA. You'll find tasty bread, sweet pastries, and lots more. Very nice: the overnight oats, the homemade kombucha, and the lunch menu. Open daily until 3.30pm.

Gartenstrasse 9, 10115 Mitte, freabakery.de

Kopps

Vegan fine dining, so not very suitable to smaller wallets. Maybe you could take the parents ... This might be one for your bucket list: it offers the best vegan food in town, promise!

Linienstrasse 94, 10119 Mitte, kopps-berlin.de

Momos

At Momos, you can order a variety of vegetarian dumplings. Opt for the menu of sixteen pieces, which gives you one of each, or make your own combinations. They also serve a tasty dumpling soup. And yes, it might sound odd, but there are even dessert dumplings.

Chausseestrasse 2, 10155 Mitte, momos-berlin.de

The Sanctuary Berlin

In a city full of cakes and cookies, it can be hard to find a bakery with great vegan options. But this is your safe zone: a beautiful Italian vegan bakery. And the coffee is excellent.

Torstrasse 175, 10115 Mitte / Prenzlauer Berg, thesanctuaryberlin.com

Café Neue Liebe

Once, this café served both vegetarian and vegan dishes, but it went fully vegan. So there's no need to ask if they can omit the cheese or honey. They serve beautiful dishes that taste great too.

Rykestrasse 42, 10405 Prenzlauer Berg, insta @cafe.neue.liebe

Froindlichst

Burgers, bowls, pizza, and burritos: this is the best place for vegan street food — but indoors. In weekends, they serve breakfast too.

Immanuelkirchstrasse 31, 10405 Prenzlauer Berg, froindlichst.com

1990 Vegan Living

Maybe not the first vegan restaurant in Berlin, but it certainly is a classic. Come here for vegan Vietnamese tapas, either inside or pick a table on the pavement.

Krossener Strasse 19, 10245 Friedrichshain, restaurant-1990.de

Secret Garden

This vegan sushi restaurant has the same owners as 1990 Vegan Living. The menu for two is very good, or alternatively, select some sushi and top it off with a main course.

Warschauer Strasse 33, 10243 Friedrichshain, secretgardenberlin.com

Vöner

More than twenty years ago, Vöner offered Berlin its first vegan döner. This manufacturer now delivers to food trucks around the country, but you can also visit their own little place in one of the nicest areas of Friedrichshain. Their vegan Currywurst with chips is another favourite.

Boxhagener Strasse 56, 10245 Friedrichshain, voener.de

Blumenthal

Surrounded by greenery and bathing in light, this beautiful vegetarian haven is a great spot for some relaxation. The tables and chairs remind us of our school days, but the food doesn't! From their beautiful counter, they serve delicious lunch, cocktails, and cakes.

Engeldamm 44, 10179 Kreuzberg, blumental-berlin.de

Amaize

Not really a restaurant, but this small place dedicated to corn is definitely worth a visit. Indulge in corn on the cob or a bowl of corn soup and yes, there's popcorn too.

Zossener Strasse 20, 10961 Kreuzberg

C+ Bakery

This must be one of the most colourful spots in town. They have an amazing selection of cakes, all vegan and most are gluten free. Cinnamon buns are their specialty. Every now and then, they host karaoke sessions, workshops, and a wide range of events, including

queer comedy and astrology &
tarot. Sounds interesting, right?

*Falckensteinstrasse 35, 10997 Kreuzberg,
insta @cplusbakery*

Alaska Berlin

A very cosy vegan bar, serving
a selection of Spanish tapas.
It is open for dinner until late.
Combine the snacks and tapas
and you'll leave satisfied.

*Reuterstrasse 85, 12053 Neukölln, insta @
alaska_berlin*

Middle

In spite of its name, this bistro
and cocktail bar is tucked away in
Neukölln close to U-bahn station
Boddinstrasse. The vegetarian
Levantine menu is short but
excellent. They serve the best
hummus and harissa in town!
The cocktails are great too.

*Mainzer Strasse 39, 12053 Neukölln,
middleberlin.com*

Miss Vegan

A nicely decorated restaurant
serving vegan food of the
healthy kind, so expect a lot of
vegetables. The Asian, mainly
Vietnamese, menu offers plenty
of options. Satisfying in every
way.

*Marburger Strasse 15, 10789 Charlottenburg,
miss-vegan.de*

NON-FOOD

Veja

The iconic sneakers with the V
are made of used plastic bottles
and organic materials. The vegan
collection (not all of them are)
is extensive. You will have a hard
time choosing your next favourite
pair. There are five Veja stores
in the world, with their shop in
Berlin as one of the first.

*Alte Schönhauser Strasse 42, 10119 Mitte,
veja-store.com*

Go to DearGoods for clothes
and accessories that you'll
keep for life (or at least for a
very long time). Everything
is animal friendly, so no
leather, wool, or silk is used.
And it's friendly to humans
too: everything is fair trade.
Brands include Armedangels,
fremdformat, Greenbomb, and
Recolution.

Rosenthaler Strasse 19, 10119 Mitte /
Schivelbeiner Strasse 34, 10439 Prenzlauer
Berg, deargoods.com

OUTSIDE OF BERLIN

There are a billion things you could do around Berlin. As mentioned before, especially in summer, Berliners like going to a nearby lake. Our favourites to go for a swim are Krumme Lanke, Schlachtensee, or Wannsee. Luckily, Berlin has many more but these three are accessible by public transport. Some can get a little crowded, but it all depends on the season and weather. Check page 32 for more info.

Beelitz-Heilstätten

baumundzeit.de

This former sanatorium's abandoned site is famous among photographers and explorers. Beelitz, a small town about an hour by train from Berlin Hauptbahnhof, is mostly famous for strawberries and asparagus, but that's not why you'd want to visit. Firstly, bring a camera; the site is great for taking some of the coolest pictures. And secondly, there is a walkway through the treetops, forty metres above ground, with great views. Entrance to the site is around 15 euros.

Potsdam

potsdam-tourism.com

What do *Grand Budapest Hotel* and *Inglorious Basterds* have in common? Technically, not much. But both were filmed in Potsdam, at Babelsberg Film Studios. And the city carries a lot of history. Potsdam is home to Schloss Sanssouci, a grand castle. During the Cold War, Potsdam's Glienicke Bridge was the place where eastern and western spies were exchanged. A Dutch quarter was built in the middle of the 18th century, at the time, home to craftsmen that had left the Netherlands to work for the King. It feels like walking around the canals in Amsterdam. There is a lot of European history to be found, as well as plenty of venues to eat and drink. From Berlin Hauptbahnhof, Potsdam is around 45 minutes by train.

Spreewald

spreewald.com

This forest is ideal if you want to spend the day immersed in nature (too much clubbing, perhaps?), and Spreewald is vast. Good starting points are the villages of Lübbenau, Lübben, or Lehde. You can book a boat trip in one of the villages and just go for the views. But there are endless options for activities in Spreewald. You can rent a kayak and paddle the day away, go cycling, or hiking. About thirty minutes by train from Berlin Hauptbahnhof.

Sachsenhausen Memorial and Museum

Strasse der Nationen 22, 16515 Oranienburg, sachsenhausen-sbg.de

If you want to delve into the history of World War II, you might want to consider visiting Sachsenhausen. In this concentration camp, already built in 1936, more than 200,000 people were interned. Jewish people, but also many of Sinti and Roma descent. Sachsenhausen can be reached in 45 minutes by S-Bahn or train from Berlin. Free for under 26s.

Dresden

dresden.de

Those interested in history should visit Dresden. The city was heavily bombed by British and American forces during World War II. And it was rebuilt in no-time , giving it an 'old' look. There are several interesting museums, among which a few dedicated to authors such as Erich Kästner and Józef Ignacy Kraszewski, and a beautiful museum of modern art. Under two hours by train from Berlin Hauptbahnhof.

Leipzig

leipzig.travel, leipzig.de

This lively student town is home to several universities, including one of the oldest in the country. Leipzig has much more to offer than just its famous St. Nicholas Church, where protests for the reunification of Germany took place in the 80s. There are lots of parks and green spots too, as well as a vibrant nightlife. Some say Leipzig has more cool credentials than Berlin, go check it out for yourself! Just one hour by train from Berlin Hauptbahnhof.

INDEX

ABOUT THE AUTHORS

Fritz Ali Hansen

Fritz is a Berlin-based musician and songwriter. In 2023 he was bass player with The Leftovers. His parents have ignited his lifelong passion for music, which he implements into both his music and his DJ sets, which he performs at various underground venues in Berlin. (Check insta @fritzalihansen for his latest releases.)

Tosca Bego

Like her sister Fenna, Tosca partially grew up in Berlin. She loves the museums, the bookshops, the amazing craft stores, and the local food. For Tosca, the best snack to have in Berlin is a *Zimtschnecke* (cinnamon bun), washed down with a Club Mate.

Fenna Bego

Fenna, who was partially raised in Berlin, is now studying in the the Dutch city of Groningen. She returns to her beloved Berlin and her old friends as often as she can. For Fenna, the city is a perfect blend of art, history, delicious food, and an amazing nightlife.

Elijah Rhode

Model, skateboarder and student, not necessarily in that order, Elijah is also a great connoisseur of local streetwear labels. He divides his time between Berlin and the Dutch city of Rotterdam.

WHY SHOULD I GO TO BERLIN
the city you definitely need to
visit before you turn 30

Published in 2024 by mo'media
P.O. Box 359, 3000 AJ Rotterdam,
The Netherlands, momedia.nl

Concept
mo'media

Text and address selection
Fritz Ali Hansen, Fenna Bego,
Tosca Bego, Elijah Rhode, and
Petra de Hamer

Art direction and illustration design
Jelle F. Post

Editing
Ezra van Wilgenburg

Photography
Petra de Hamer, Vincent van den
Hoogen, David in den Bosch,
mo'media BV, and others

Special thanks to
Maaike van Steekelenburg, Hidde Bego,
Lotte Leeuwis, and Eva van den Berg

(m)

Copyright © mo'media BV, 2024

Why Should I Go To Berlin
ISBN 978 94 93 338 074
NUR 510

Disclaimer
The points of interested mentioned in this
travel guide have been selected by the
authors. None of them have been paid for
inclusion in this book: the *Why Should I Go To*
book series is entirely ad-free.

Publisher's Note
Every effort has been made to ensure that
the information in this book is accurate at
the time of going to press. The publisher
welcomes any information or suggestions for
correction or improvement. Please send us
an e-mail at info@momedia.nl or a DM on
Instagram.

whyshouldigoto